W9-CYA-734

1

The 60's Star Trek
Special Effects On A Budget

When Roddenberry sold Desilu Studios on the idea of STAR TREK, he luckily had access to one of the best special effects houses. The Howard Anderson Company began consulting with Roddenberry even as he was preparing his script, "The Cage," for production. Rolland "Bud" Brooks, the Desilu supervising art director, assigned Matt Jeffries to work on STAR TREK. Brooks knew that Jeffries was an aviation enthusiast and would probably take to this material. A member of the Aviation Writers Association, Matt Jeffries had collected a lot of design material relating to NASA and the defense industry. He reportedly used that material as well as example of ships used in Flash Gordon and Buck Rogers as exactly what they wanted to avoid on STAR TREK.

When Matt Jeffries met with the creator of STAR TREK to discuss designs for the Enterprise, he recalled (in THE MAKING OF STAR TREK by Stephen E. Whitfield and Gene Roddenberry) being told, "We're a hundred and fifty, maybe two hundred years from now. Out in deep space, on the equivalent of a cruiser-size spaceship. We don't know what the motive power is, but I don't want to see any trails of fire. No streaks of smoke, no jet intakes, rocket exhaust, or anything like that. We're not going to Mars, or any of that sort of limited thing. It will be like a deep space exploration vessel, operating throughout our galaxy. We'll be going to stars and planets that nobody has named yet. I don't care how you do it, but make it look like it's got power."

In the March 1987 issue of CINEFANTASTIQUE, Jeffries stated, "I think the first time we had a review, I probably had a hundred different sketches. There were certain elements of some that we liked and certain elements of others that we liked and we kinda tossed the rest aside and began to assemble things with the elements that had some appeal to us." One possible design had a spherical primary hull instead of the saucer-shaped hull. At one point the design of the Enterprise was viewed as being upside down from what was finally settled on.

The strange design of the ship makes it difficult to tell top from bottom (the identification numbers are the only real clue). This is why you will still see photos of the starship printed upside down in books and magazines, even twenty-five years later.

CONSTRUCTION OF THE ENTERPRISE

After Matt Jeffries came up with a design of the Enterprise which Roddenberry liked, he oversaw its construction and made sure that what was brought to the screen didn't sell short the imaginative possibilities of his story. Walter M. "Matt" Jeffries worked with Desilu art director Pato Guzman on the design of the Enterprise. The fourteen foot model was constructed by Don Loos of Van Nuys. As it was, science fiction for television up to that point had been in black and white. Bringing color to such images brought its own share of challenges.

Three models of the Enterprise were built: a four inch version, a three-foot model and the highly detailed fourteen foot Enterprise which today hangs in Washington, D.C., in the Smithsonian. The fourteen foot Enterprise was constructed by a technician at NASA, Don Loos, who ordinarily made models for wind tunnel tests. He said he got a lot of strange looks from his co-workers when he was building that model.

The ten foot diameter saucer shaped primary hull was made out of plastic, as was the lower cigar-shaped primary hull. The windows were made out of ground glass, which gave an even distribution of light when filmed. The lower hull had a large hole in the bottom which fit over a pipe upon which the model was mounted for filming. The engines and engine pylons were made from balsa wood and had tiny pins protruding from them which could be used to hook the model to wires and suspend it from the ceiling. The interior of the model was a mass if wires.

The fourteen foot model was used for all shots of the Enterprise when it was moving left to right on the screen. The reason for this is that the opposite side of the fourteen foot model had places where power cables emerged from the pylons and the primary hull. Ordinarily for shots of the Enterprise moving from right to left they employed the three foot model made by Matt Jeffries.

THE DIFFICULTIES OF MODEL MAKING

It was possible to use the fourteen foot model going in the opposite direction but it required flopping the image, and that meant putting decals on backwards so that when reversed they would read forwards. As the series progressed and the larger model was enhanced, interior and exterior lights were added. The nacelles were also customized by putting motors in the front of them so that spinning, flashing multicolored lights could be seen in the nose of each of them. This was particularly evident in the third season.

Recalling the difficulties inherent in model-making in the sixties, Jeffries told CINEFANTASTIQUE, "The most difficult thing about doing the show was that we did not have today's materials to play with. We were working with ordinary construction materials. Even Fiberglass molding and that kind of stuff was still relatively new and there weren't many people around who could do it. Nowadays you've got all kinds of wild-eyed plastics and molding stuff—none of that was available to us then."

THE
SPECIAL
EFFECTS
OF
TREK

OTHER PIONEER BOOKS

Designed and Edited by Hal Schuster
with assistance from David Lessnick

THE SPECIAL EFFECTS OF TREK

OF TREK

By James Van Hise

Books for the entertainment buyer

PIONEER

Library of Congress Cataloging-in-Publication Data
James Van Hise, 1949—
    The Special Effects of Trek

    1.   The Special Effects of Trek (television)
 I. Title

Published by Pioneer Books, Inc., 5715 N. Balsam Rd., Las Vegas, NV, 89130.

First Printing, 1993

The way the Enterprise was shown flying through space towards the camera began by setting the model up on its mount, three feet in the air on a set of narrow tracks. The camera then moves towards the model, turning and tilting as it approaches the model. This creates the illusion of movement combined with the more limited movements of the model on its track.

One of the most popular special effects was the Transporter, which remained consistent over the three seasons. This was done by making a matte of an actor standing perfectly still and using that to pull a matte which fit the outline of the actor. This was accomplished by first filming an actor standing in the Transporter. The camera continued filming as the actor stepped out of camera range leaving the camera filming the empty set. The footage of the actor walking away was edited out.

TRANSPORTING AND PHASING

On another piece of film, a mask was shot which perfectly matched the outline of the actor just filmed. This film is then superimposed on the Transporter film creating an image of the Transporter with a hole in it which matches the silhouette of the actor. Then aluminum shavings were photographed through a powerful light on one of the mattes and it was composited with the image of the actor. The actor seem to disappear amid a strange effect.

The film of the actor is faded out first leaving the sparkle which is then dissolved out of the scene as well. The result is the Transporter effect. This is all reversed in making a person seem to reappear after appearing elsewhere. The only time this varied was in the second season episode "Mirror, Mirror" when they deliberately wanted to show an alternate version of the Transporter effect for the parallel universe version of the Enterprise.

The phaser beams were always made the same way, even though the colors on the phasers changed once in awhile depending on which optical house was doing them and whether they had been told what color to make them. The phasers were animated, a frame at a time, using a series of drawings. Each was slightly longer than the other, superimposed over either a space craft model or over a close-up of someone holding a hand phaser (or in the case of "Where No Man Has Gone Before," a phaser rifle, which was used only in that episode).

When the first pilot, "The Cage," was filmed, Roddenberry personally contacted the special effects people to fine tune what he saw filmed. He insisted that they eliminate the thick matte line around the crew members as they're transported. Making certain that an effect has no matte lines is very time consuming but the end result is well worth it. He also wanted a more subtle sparkle in the Transporter effect as opposed to the heavy sparkle effect the optical house had included.

WHITE OR BLUE?

When the crew materialized on the surface of a planet, he wanted the same color effect used on each rather than the assortment of colors which had been added to the sparkles. He also wanted the crew members to slowly dissolve with a slight flickering of color rather than using a solid color. Regarding the Enterprise, Roddenberry insisted that there be no movement of the stars as the spaceship moves across the screen.

For special effects requiring composites, the scenes with the Enterprise were filmed in black and white. Then once the composite was made, color would be filtered into it using an Oxberry optical printer. This is why over the three seasons the color of the Enterprise changed from show to show. Sometimes it appeared to be white while other times the starship was clearly blue, such as in the first season show "Space Seed."

The fact that different optical houses were working on STAR TREK sometimes added to this rotating color effect on the Enterprise. It was in the third season that the Enterprise was most often seen as an off-white, except when stock footage was used. This created other contradictions as the Enterprise model was revised over the three years, the changes being most notable on the front and back of the engine nacelles.

In order to show the Enterprise moving through a star field, they'd splatter white cards with black paint and put them on an optical printer, doing multiple passes until they had forty-five feet of moving stars they could loop. The opening titles which showed the Enterprise flying close by the camera were done using the four inch Enterprise model. The camera dollied in on the model, shooting it one frame at a time with a camera hanging from a boom. The final result made it appear that the Enterprise was flying rapidly towards the camera.

THE OLD PAN-AND-TILT

The larger models of the Enterprise were photographed by mounting them on a pole which was connected to a pan-and-tilt tripod head so that they could move the model around in the shot when necessary. The pole was sheathed in a blue material to make it blend in with the blue screen it was photographed against. The pan-and-tilt head had to be operated manually by an operator covered in a blue tarp.

Today such movements are controlled by computers which move models according to operator instructions typed into them. The camera photographing the Enterprise was mounted on a dolly which had its own pan-and-tilt tripod. The speed of the ship could be enhanced by both the camera movements and the use of an eighteen millimeter lens, which would also give the shots a greater depth of field perspective.

While an average TV show of the mid-sixties used maybe one optical effect every other episode, STAR TREK was using up to twenty per episode. Ordinarily opticals had to be planned far in advance because it took upwards of ten weeks between ordering and delivery. So Roddenberry and his team visited optical houses and suggested ways to cut the time factor. This created some raised eyebrows and ruffled feathers, but it worked.

Said Roddenberry at the time, "The fact new and cheaper methods were developed to improve upon something that had been done a certain way for twenty or thirty years is a definite tribute to the unusual group of people we have at STAR TREK. STAR TREK is probably, physically, the most difficult television series that's ever been done. While I bow low and smile when people compliment me, the unsung heroes of the show are people like Bob Justman with his intimate knowledge of sets, costs, production facilities, and so on; Matt Jeffries with his uncanny talent for bringing in impossible sets on impossible budgets, every time; and Eddie Milkis, who is an absolute whiz in the post-production area, practically with opticals; Bill Theiss who is a genius at costume design; in fact, virtually every member of the production crew.

GENE GETS WHAT HE WANTS

These are the people who have made STAR TREK what it is. These are the people who keep us in business. Television is not only a creative art (we dignify it with that term) but it's also a very, very tough business."

In March 1966, after NBC had given a go-ahead on the series, Roddenberry had further ideas regarding the special effects. Besides some changes he wanted to make on the models, he also had other suggestions about the special effects footage already completed. "Also needed is a meeting on additional stock footage shooting—this get-together coming some time after we've got enough outlines in to make a reasonable projection. *Important,* we should also at this meeting review how we liked past stock footage and plan to revise and correct wherever we feel it is indicated.

For example, in STAR TREK #2 [A reference to the second pilot, "Where No Man Has Gone Before,"] on some of the U.S.S. Enterprise approaching planet footage, I felt the time-speed-distance perspective was considerably off." Roddenberry also wanted a search made regarding what stock footage was available from NASA and the Air Force. Such footage was used in the first season episode "Tomorrow Is Yesterday" and the second season episode "Assignment: Earth," the only two stories set in the 1960's.

After working on the first seven episodes of the series, the special effects chores were split with Linwood Dunn's Film Effects of Hollywood due to the demands of producing special effects for a weekly show. The special effects crews would work all night in order to have footage to show Roddenberry the following morning when he came into the studio. It had to be done in this way because the compositing of the optical effects was the last thing done in an episode in preparing it for airing.

ENTER EDDIE MILKIS

By the tenth episode the special effects work was running so late that episodes were backed up. Matters became so critical at one point early in the first season that episodes were being completed on Saturday which would air the following Thursday. This was when Eddie Milkis was brought in as the post-production supervisor to untangle things and see that such matters were completed more quickly and without as many problems and delays.

At the effects house run by Linwood Dunn, Albert Whitlock, the now legendary matte painter, painted some of STAR TREK's more memorable matte's. But sometimes there wasn't time to get a matte painting, as in the third season episode "The Cloud Minders" when Matt Jeffries had a miniature made to use instead of a matte painting. The floating sky city was hung in front of a backdrop and the miniature city sat on a spun glass cloud. Since it was always filmed in a long shot, it worked. A matte painting was employed to show the planet's surface far below when Kirk and the others look down over the edge of the city after a man commits suicide by leaping off. The effect of distance is well achieved, even though it flashes on the screen for only a couple of seconds.

One of the more commonplace special effects in the series was the view screen. It was so commonly used that people took it for granted, but it was also one of the more complicated effects and it added to the lengthy post-production time on the show. The stages of the effect began with first shooting the view screen on the set and then turning that film over to the optical house. A black area the exact size of the viewing area is then masked out on another piece of film.

A second mask is made on yet another piece of film of everything in the frame except the area already masked out on the previous piece of film. The original film of the view screen is rephotographed with the matte in place blocking out the screen area. This results in a piece of film with an empty spot, or hoe, where the viewing area is. Then using the second mask, the special effects to be shown on the view screen is rephotographed on the second mask which had been made of the original piece of view screen film. Now the two pieces of new film are combined in an optical printer and rephotographed onto a third piece of film so that the two pieces have been blended into one seamless whole.

THE ELEVATOR AND SHUTTLE BAY

Sometimes the unusual effects seen on the view screen of the Enterprise were managed by using what is now called a cloud tank, a process which was used as far back as the early 1930's. A tank of clear fluid would have colored dyes poured into it and the movement of the dyes in the liquid often created unusual patterns and color combinations which looked great on film.

The elevator on the Enterprise had its own logical use of special effects which was outlined to the crew by producer Bob Justman in an August 1966 memo. "It would be greatly appreciated that any time we have a shot in an elevator where we have a light effect to indicate movement and speed of movement, in addition to indicating the speed-up of movement as the elevator starts off, we also indicate a slowdown of movement before the elevator stops and the doors open. We have got to be able to give the Special Effects Man or the Electrician working the light effect a correct cue to start working that light effect, so that we can believe that the elevator is stopping prior to the opening of its doors."

The three foot model of the Enterprise was generally used in battle scenes when the Enterprise would appear on screen with another ship. It was after Linwood Dunn took over a lot of the effects work, including most shots involving the Enterprise, that the shuttle bay was constructed. This is why the shuttle didn't even exist in the earliest episodes.

The star fields which Linwood used were achieved simply by poking holes in large sheets of black paper and putting lights behind them. To make sure the stars didn't all appear identical, he put colored gels and diffusion screens behind some.

MASTER MODEL MAKER

Linwood Dunn had his own optical printer which had been built in his ships. His precision three-head contact printer enabled him to create the mattes and color masters they required in order to produce the final composite shots.

Not all of the special effects chores were handled by the Howard A. Anderson Company and Linwood Dunn. While they photographed the effects, model work was sometimes done by others for reasons of time and budget.

The Romulan ship which was used the first season episode, "Balance of Terror", was designed and constructed by the famous model-builder Wah Chang. Wah Chang is legendary and worked on such film projects as THE SEVEN FACES OF DR. LAO, THE TIME MACHINE and THE OUTER LIMITS. For the original STAR TREK series, Chang built the Tricorder, Communicator, the Gorn costume, the head of the phony Balok in "The Corbomite Maneuver," as well as the Romulan ship.

Recalls Chang, "I did it in my studio at home and didn't get any screen credit because of not belonging to the union at that time. All that time before this, being part owner of Project Unlimited, I had been doing camera work, modeling, special effects and design. I probably should have gone to the cameraman's union or the prop-maker's, but being the owner of the business, I wasn't required. So when I started doing work on STAR TREK, I would drive into the studio, get a preliminary script which might indicate a little bit what the monster was going to do and so on, and I'd go back home and do either a drawing or a rough clay model. Then I'd drive back to the studio and show it to the directors, or Roddenberry or Gene Coon and they'd okay it and I'd go back and finish it."

FROM DRAWING TO REALITY

One of the drawings which Chang did was of the Tricorder. The drawing looks exactly like the finished model. He also came up with the final look of the communicator and built that. His work on the phaser was much more minimal and not as all-encompassing.

"I really didn't design the phaser so much as sort of modify it and make it better. So I can't take credit for the phaser. In fact, that was so long ago that I don't remember too much about the phaser, but the Communicator and the Tricorder I did completely from scratch, as well as a lot of the monsters they used.

As with most things Wah Chang made for STAR TREK in the sixties, he had something less than two weeks from the time he received the assignment to make the Romulan ship, until it was due. Chang described the original model as having been about eighteen inches across and explained that the bird of prey design was added later at the studio. The model was made of plaster and was apparently destroyed after this episode was filmed.

This ship only appeared in one other episode, "The Deadly Years," and all of those scenes were stock footage from "Balance Of Terror." For some reason, in the third season in "The Enterprise Incident," the Romulans used Klingon ships. The bird of prey design which graces the bottom of the original Romulan ship was transposed. The description of it was used on the STAR TREK movies when describing the redesigned Klingon ships seen in STAR TREK III, IV and V and VI.

PARTNERS AGAIN

Chang reteamed with Gene Warren and they opened up another studio called Excelsior. Although Chang only worked on the first two years of STAR TREK, he became more directly involved with the special effects during that time as well. "When Gene Warren and I had Excelsior," Chang recalls, "we sometimes worked with the Howard Anderson Company, which did a lot of the optical effects on STAR TREK using the big model. We reworked some small models, put lights in and so forth, but mostly on STAR TREK it was working on monsters and so forth."

Other props and certain on-the-set mechanical effects were handled by Jim Rugg. In the first season, for "City On The Edge of Forever," it was Rugg who pieced together the set-up using antique vacuum tubes which enabled Spock to view the material his tricorder had recorded from the Guardian of Forever. In "Operation: Annihilate," the blob parasites of Deneva were made by Jim Rugg (in collaboration with Wah Chang) so that the rubber props could adhere to certain parts of the set by means of unseen electro-magnets.

The blobs were cast from Plastiflex, a translucent flexible molding material. When inlaid with a strip of metal, the electromagnet would just be turned off when the blob was supposedly hit by a phaser blast and had to drop from its position. In the scene when one "flies" across the room and hits Spock in the back, one of the things was connected to the end of a line on a fishing pole. In one of take, Rugg's aim was low and the blob his Spock in the butt.

For the second season episode "The Changeling," Rugg built a robot-like device four feet high. It was wired with a complex array of lights, motors, relays and a voice-activated circuit which enabled certain lights to work in synchronization with the recorded voice that Nomad used. However, the voice heard in the episode was clearly rerecorded and looped in post-production. For tight shots, Nomad was moved along the floor on a dolly track which gave it a floating effect. When the bottom needed to be seen, Nomad was on wires suspended from a monorail attached to the ceiling of the set.

INVENTIVENESS AND SLIDING DOORS

Another example of Jim Rugg's inventiveness can be seen in "The Trouble With Tribbles." Some of the tribbles had balloons in them with a hidden hose connected to it. The hose pumped air into it which made it to appear to be alive and pulsating . Others had wind-up spring motors in them to make them move while the large ones had the innards of mechanical toy dogs so that the tribble would be able to move on its own for as long as its batteries held out. Rugg was also in charge of maintaining the various working devices on the bridge, such as view screens which broke down under the rigors of daily use.

The automatic doors on STAR TREK was a different kind of special effect. Although they were mechanical in nature, they were operated by a prop man who opened them on cue. The doors were linked with cables so that pulling on one cable opened the other door at the same time. A missed cue meant that the actor walked into a closed door. It wasn't long after this that electronic doors started appearing in stores with a pressure pad to open them when someone stepped on it. We take those for granted today.

A different sort of on-the-set special effect was employed in "Shore Leave" to represent gun fire when an airplane straffs a fleeing crewman. This was managed with what is called a "nail board" which was hidden under the sand. A row of nails in a board has a squib (a tiny explosive) tied to each nail. A common connector links the nails to a battery and the connector is raked along the nails, setting off the squibs one after the other.

One of the best known models built for the original STAR TREK, and whose design continues to this day, is the Klingon ship. The Klingon ship was designed by Matt Jeffries and Stephen E. Whitfield. The model was constructed of balsa wood, a little plastic and epoxy. The ship measured about two and a half feet in length and had the same rigging set-up as the Enterprise: the hole underneath for a dowel to support it, and small pins on the top for support by wires.

MORE SPECIAL EFFECTS

However, it wasn't as large a model as the Enterprise and it only weighed five pounds. It had no lights or interior wiring at all. The lights were either painted on white or were black decals swiped from several hobby kits. There was only one Klingon model built as when more than one was shown it was duplicated optically, such as in "The Enterprise Incident."

"The Doomsday Machine" was a high spot of the second season. The episode made some of the most extensive use of special effects of any episode that season. Those effects included a second starship, the battered Constellation, which was actually an AMT Enterprise model with the NCC-1701 decal rearranged to read NCC-1017 and a lot of burn marks on the plastic surface.

The use of the plastic model is apparent in scenes when you can actually see the nacelles on the model shaking, as the regular spaceship models used on the show had been carved from wood. This was not the first time an AMT Enterprise kit had been used to cut corners. In "The Trouble With Tribbles," when Kirk is inside the space station, the Enterprise we can see in the distance through a viewport is another AMT model.

Mike Minor, who worked as a production illustrator on STAR TREK—THE MOTION PICTURE and STAR TREK II: THE WRATH OF KHAN, first became associated with STAR TREK during the third season of the original television series. He sold some astronomical paintings he had done which were used as set decorations in the Enterprise. Then the post-production associate producer, Eddie Milkis, called him and asked if he could come up with an alien creature they needed. "I said I'd love to and it turned out to be a show called 'Spectre of the Gun.' They needed the Melkotian, which was some kind of a floating, disembodied entity that didn't have a corporeal form, but we still had to show something on the screen rather than just some flickering lights.

GETTING TECHNICAL

I came up with a miniature head which was a brain case, two eyes set deep into skull sockets, no nose and no mouth because I reasoned that they'd have evolved away from mandibles or having to eat since there was no body. It was simply done for the effect of the moment. I cast it up in foam, which I'd never done before. I went down and saw the people at the Don Post Studios and bought my first can of latex. I sculpted it in clay, made a negative female plaster mold and developed the latex into a half-inch thick mass, which is flexible.

It was shot over at one of the optical houses which worked on the show. We shot it against black and put pingpong balls in the eyes, cut cat-like slit pupils and put high intensity tensor beams behind it and put a star filter over the lens. This was shot and this image was literally double-exposed over a cloud effect on the stage. It made about three appearances in the show. So that was the first on-screen effect that I did anywhere."

One of the best special effects entries in the third season was "The Tholian Web." This doesn't have any of the elements which earmarked most of the third season scripts as it is intelligent, suspenseful and well-handled from all angles. The special effects were so outstanding that this episode was nominated for an Emmy in that category, and received a special "close-up" in that week's TV GUIDE featuring a photo of the Enterprise—printed upside down.

Mike Minor worked on this episode, and of it he recalled that it had an optical bill of ninety thousand dollars. When he was brought in, he stated that, "They'd written the show and had already shot it, and they had seventeen cuts planned for the show showing the web of energy being woven about the Enterprise by the enemy craft, the Tholians. I did my first storyboards for this show and it got me into optical houses. I was working with Frank Van der Veer's optical house".

THE ERSATZ GEODESIC DOME

"We shot the models, which had been produced elsewhere, on a little stage at a place down on La Brea. These elements were shot against black velvet so that we could flop the images and have a ship going left to right, from the bottom right to the top corner. Or, the image of one ship moving diagonally across the screen could be positived with the image of a smaller ship moving diagonally left to right, right to left or up and down.

We built up a series of grid movements which describe an ersatz geodesic dome. In a sense, it wasn't a true geodesic dome because the triangles which make up a geodesic dome have tangency but they don't line up in parallel bandings; everything's moving off in tangents. But for plot simplicity in getting the job done we simply had them moving in parallel movements, left to right and right to left. We never pulled back wide, which I wanted to do, and show the whole ship being dragged through space with this spherical dome of energy about it.

"Once they shot the model, I projected the shots a frame at a time onto a white surface with a rotoscope set-up. Then I put pencil marks where the ship moved and traced and advanced each frame. I created the cel-like cartoon animation using black lines for the grid. Each shot in the episode showed a partially completed grid with one line being animated across the field as though by the Tholian ship. I shot those by pulling a white card frame-by-frame and revealing the black line underneath. A black and white negative of this resulted in a black background with a clear line on the film which was used to create an animation burn in. But that work lasted me for about four months."

The Tholian commander which appeared in the episode was constructed by Minor out of Plexiglas entity on a camera stand, lit internally against a field of tin foil. "They played with the image and did mattes off of it—black and white mattes, separations and color substitutions. They added real strong saturating colors so that it got stranger and stranger.

POSITIVE AND NEGATIVE

By pulling a black and white matte, positive and negative (a positive image of the creature and a negative image of the background), you could do separations and therefore throw more color into the background and less color into the figure. Or, let color seep into it as frames went on, and let it dissolve into colors in the optical printer so that the characters went through various sheens of color and harmonies which didn't really exist."

"He was supposed to be a crystalline structure, silicon based," Minor explained. "I think there was a script mention about that but I'm not sure. I took that to mean that he was prismatic, with a rigid exoskeleton body scan. All of this was being done for speed and time and you're always working against time and money—that's where you make your living in this town. You gain either a reputation for or against you about how you use your time and money to the best effect. That's the game and also the pressure."

The direction on this episode was particularly good, particularly the touch of the fish-eye lens used on point of view shots when showing what an insane person was seeing. The use of the environmental suits was also a nice touch. Although it's not as apparent on the TV screen as it is when seen on a large screen, the space helmets did not use glass but rather a very fine mesh wire screen which photographed quite convincingly. It also made it easier for the actors to breathe, a problem common in space suits used on other films and TV series.

These days such full body costumes employ a "cool suit" worn underneath them such as race car drivers use, but this is only a recent addition. When Leonard Nimoy wore a full body space suit (with a sealed helmet) in STAR TREK: THE MOTION PICTURE, he was left unattended at one point, hanging in the air, and fainted from the heat built up in the costume. What made "The Tholian Web" special was the use of animation as the small Tholian ships painstakingly constructed the web around the Enterprise, which was actually done via animation.

THE OLD EFFECTS STILL HOLD UP TODAY

The alien ship from "The Tholian Web" was simply balsa wood and sheet plastic, with a couple pieces of adhesive crosshatched silver foil slapped on the back. This same kind of silver foil was used on hand phasers and other implements. Both the Klingon and the Tholian ship were painted a flat military gray.

Although today the special effects of the sixties STAR TREK are sometimes referred to as being "crude," this is because they're being compared to the multi-million dollar effects seen in the STAR TREK motion pictures. Of course the sometimes grainy looking spacecraft will come off as second best compared to the work of Douglas Trumbull or Industrial Light & Magic.

However, aside from the advantage of a bigger budget and more time, the technology had advanced ten years since the TV series had been canceled when STAR TREK—THE MOTION PICTURE hit theater screens. Even so, the resolution and integrity of those old special effects is remarkably good. The matte paintings hold up even when projected on screens ten feet in diameter.

For a television series which was blazing new trails in special effects twenty-five years ago, STAR TREK continues to be a rich source of wonder and entertainment, no matter how you look at it.

2

The Motion Picture
The Effects Become The Star

―――――

        " The climate had been created by STAR WARS, which had been released in 1977," Leonard Nimoy quite rightly observed some years later. "We were very grateful for STAR WARS for having established that climate because I am convinced that it was the success of STAR WARS in 1977 that caused somebody at Paramount to say, 'Hey, we have one of those. It's called STAR TREK. Let's do it.' But that STAR WARS atmosphere had to be dealt with because it was an atmosphere of a very physical special effect, large-looking motion picture as compared to what the STAR TREK episodes offered which was a lot of times spent with actors interacting with each other.

Nimoy went on, "In STAR TREK: THE MOTION PICTURE we spent a lot of time staring at the view screen on which later would be a lot of sizable special effects. So the climate was problematic. I think it was a tastefully presented and produced film. Obviously a very well crafted film, and certainly Paramount showed that they were serious about making as fine a picture as possible. They bit the bullet financially. We started out with a $15 million budget and let it expand, hoping for the best, to $45 million."

Three days before ST—TMP went before the cameras, on August 4, 1978, Gene Roddenberry had stated in an interview, "Let me also say, though, that it's still going to be STAR TREK. We didn't take a look at STAR WARS or CLOSE ENCOUNTERS and say, 'Oh, wow, we've got to change and be all opticals and that sort of stuff.'" Roddenberry was clearly trapped by what Paramount wanted the film to be in light of what they thought STAR WARS was.

This is the problem with many post-STAR WARS science fiction films. Things would have been different if CLOSE ENCOUNTERS OF THE THIRD KIND was the only big sf film released in 1977-78. CE3K was being made long before STAR WARS came out, but because it followed STAR WARS by six months it was labeled a big "special effects" film even though it used those effects as a counterpoint so that they stood out in contrast by suggesting the wonders waiting in space.

―――――

MONEY TALKS

In STAR WARS, like in ST: TMP, the special effects were on screen almost constantly in one form or another. The film confounded Hollywood insiders by quickly earning more that $200 million. What Paramount never noticed was that in STAR WARS, the story is actually more important than the effects. The effects are there to enhance the script, but they are not the script's raison d'être, which is the case in STAR TREK: THE MOTION PICTURE.

Back in 1975, Walter Koenig had something very prophetic to say when he was a guest on THE TOMORROW SHOW (hosted by Tom Snyder) where he appeared along with James Doohan, DeForest Kelley and Harlan Ellison. This was before the motion picture was ever announced and they were having an academic discussion on what would happen if STAR TREK were revived. Koenig, in those pre-STAR WARS days, made the very canny observation that: "The only problem is, if it's a feature film as opposed to a made for television show, they'll decide that they have to change the thrust of it in some way, make it monsters and huge battle scenes; something that you can't get on television. You may distort the entire feeling of the show."

A year later, when the film had been announced, DeForest Kelley, in discussing Paramount's seemingly endless search for the "right script," remarked that what Paramount was looking for was a "JAWS in space." This was in 1976, one year after JAWS had been released to big box-office returns. A year later their focus would change again, and each time it would be to imitate someone else's successful idea, rather than to innovate one of their own. As it turned out, they concocted a curious combination of JAWS and STAR WARS, and it was a very unsatisfying mix.

It was this atmosphere in which ST—TMP finally went into production. When the film was officially announced at a grand press conference on March 28, 1978, the budget was a stated $15 million. This would swell enormously and special effects would be at the heart of the problems. Michael Eisner, president of Paramount at the time, stated that the visuals, "will be of extreme importance" and revealed that Robert Abel & Associates had been placed in charge of the special effects.

THE GOLDEN BOY

Abel stated in an interview with the trade publication DAILY VARIETY that two-thirds of the picture would involve opticals, special effects and animation. Robert Abel was the golden boy of the hour, a prize-winning maker of commercials whose use of special effects set the industry standard at the time for innovation. In 1978, his was one of the only companies set up specifically to specialize in the use of special optical effects, although many others were formed over the following two years to handle the increasing demands for optical effects in television and motion pictures.

An article published in the March 26, 1979 issue of NEW WEST magazine reported that besides his reputation for excellence, Robert Abel had become well known in the industry for other things as well. This included lateness and cost overruns so that some major clients had begun looking elsewhere for the kind of work Abel could provide. Abel gave Paramount an estimate of $4 million for producing the special effects then required of ST—TMP. Following rewrites on the script (which were constant throughout the production), Abel's estimate by December 1978 had swollen to $16 million, an amount greater than the entire budget for the film as stated by Paramount in March of that year.

In FANTASTIC FILMS magazine for September 1979, Robert Wise discussed what faced him when he was hired to direct STAR TREK—THE MOTION PICTURE. "I came into a situation that was already set in many ways. That's very unusual for me. I'd never worked this way before, and it was kind of a strange feeling. I'm learning to deal with it, finding ways in which I can alter things that have already been set. Since I couldn't start from scratch I've tried to upgrade things and improve them so they'll all come out looking like they belong in the same film."

The director stressed that the biggest problem he faced was the crush of time to finish the special effects. "That was our major problem. The challenge of doing the effects and getting them up there and dealing with them is no problem for me. The time I have to do them in, that everybody has to do them in, is the problem. But I want to make one point that is very important. There is nothing more important on any film than the foreground, the actors, the story. That's what we worked on like a son-of-a-gun. We had to be sure that the story we put in front of these marvelous photographic effects was going to be worthy of them and hopefully hold its own against the special photographic effects and not suffer by comparison."

THE DESIGNS OF PROBERT

While Richard Taylor was the Art Director on ST—TMP initially, he had a number of talented people working with him. One of them was Andrew Probert. Robert Abel was still in charge of the special effects when Probert was hired and the designer began his duties by reading the script in order to determine exactly what kinds of vehicles were needed. Andy Probert's first professional film work was on ST—TMP. He was hired upon the recommendation of Ralph McQuarrie. McQuarrie (the production designer on STAR WARS) had been associated with the STAR TREK II television revival in 1977 and when it was canceled he got involved with THE EMPIRE STRIKES BACK. When Paramount approached him to work on ST—TMP, McQuarrie recommended Probert. Andy Probert met with Robert Abel who liked the artist's designs and hired him a week later.

The first designs Probert worked on related to the dry-dock sequence. Mike Minor had originally designed an orbiting space dock when this same story (then titled "In Thy Image") was being crafted for the abandoned STAR TREK II television series. Probert looked over Minor's designs and reworked them. He came up with a dry-dock which was more open and less like the interior of a building.

While Richard Taylor was in charge, he assigned one designer to each type of effect in order to maintain a continuity within those effects. Dick Freeson (who worked on FORBIDDEN PLANET) came up with designs which would have given the Enterprise a "shock bubble" around the ship as well as a warp effect visible between the engine nacelles. This was discarded when Douglas Trumbull took over and most of Robert Abel's technicians and designers left the picture.

Among the vehicles Probert designed were the "Work Bees." These were small one-man contrivances designed to help get a job done in a hurry. While these weren't specifically mentioned in the script, Probert determined that since Kirk wanted the Enterprise ready in twenty-four hours rather than the two weeks scheduled, a lot of extra activity would ensue. The crafts were yellow with a black stripe, hence the bee nickname. The Work Bee was designed to be like the cab of a truck and the device could attach itself to other mechanisms which it could operate, such as for cargo-towing, laser-welding, etc.

MORE CREATIVE DESIGNS

The Travel Pod was there so that when Kirk couldn't use the off-line Transporter, there could be a scene showing the new Enterprise from Kirk and Scotty's point of view inside the Travel Pod. It was a way to show the audience exactly how new and different the redesigned Enterprise was. The Travel Pod was designed to be part of the office complex in the space dock. Gene Roddenberry wanted the pod to look like it was part of the complex until it separated, as though this would somehow surprise the audience. When Andy Probert designed the pod with a door at the back, for boarding from the complex, and a docking ring on the side for docking with standard vehicles, Roddenberry said no. He just wanted the door in the back, which meant that the pod would always have to back up to whatever it was docking with, an awkward notion at best.

Probert also did the updating of the Klingon ships. While he stuck with Joe Jennings original design from the TV show, a lot of detailing was added for the big screen. This included panels, guns and a weapons system. The bridge of the Klingon ship was designed by Probert based on his own ideas with input from Douglas Trumbull.

V'ger was originally designed by Robert Abel's crew. The intention was to show the shape of V'ger with a twenty-one inch model of the Enterprise photographed with it for scale. This idea was jettisoned when Trumbull took over. Originally though, it was decided that V'ger would be 70 kilometers long but that figure never made it into the film.

Originally the Enterprise was to have entered V'ger, explored several chambers, and then exited for the meeting with the old Voyager satellite. Although never made clear in the motion picture, V'ger never really destroyed anything. It just digitized it and broke it down into a memory pattern. Based on this concept, Mike Minor and Douglas Trumbull had conceived an ending in which not only the Enterprise is ejected when V'ger transforms, but the three Klingon ships are as well. A battle royal would have resulted. Andy Probert actually drew up some storyboards for this sequence, but it was finally abandoned for reasons of time and other constraints.

MAGICAM'S ROLE

Magicam, the special effects division of Paramount Pictures at that time, was the primary effects unit on line to work on STAR TREK when it was originally being prepped for a television revival in 1977. For that version, Magicam was going to build the space dock, the Klingon ship and space station and some other models. The Enterprise was going to be built by someone else, although Paramount actually attempted to borrow back the original model they'd donated to the Smithsonian nearly a decade before.

The Smithsonian did agree to lend Paramount the original Klingon model from the TV series. However, when plans for the TV series were canceled and the project was green lighted as a $15 million motion picture, all the work Magicam had done on models for the TV series was scrapped. Models for a feature film would need to have more detail than what could be gotten away with on a TV show. This included a fourteen foot model of V'ger which had an alligator like maw at each end. V'ger would go through many design changes before it was finally put on film.

This is when Robert Abel & Associates was hired and Richard Taylor was put in charge of all the special effects. This move took the control away from Magicam. Apparently some of the Magicam personnel considered this to be a snub and as friction developed, the more complicated the filmmaking process on ST—TMP became.

Magicam did build some of the models used in the film, including the space dock, based on a drawing by Andrew Probert. The space dock was built using half inch glass tubing which was bent into the shapes needed by an aerospace tube bender facility. The tubing had to be strong in order to support the thousands of wires running through it. The space dock took five months to complete and included fifty-six neon grids, each six by six inches, which each required three thousand volts of electricity in order to operate. So this meant that each neon panel had its own transformer with huge cables to handle all the power.

MORE THAN HE COULD HANDLE

In August 1978, it was obvious to special effects expert Douglas Trumbull that the motion picture special effects challenges were more than Robert Abel's company could handle. He went to Paramount and offered to take over the job, but Paramount turned him down. They did hire him as a special consultant some months later and he acted in that capacity January through March 1979. By then Paramount decided that Abel couldn't handle the work and put Trumbull in charge of the effects. Bob Abel's firm ceased its involvement with the motion picture Feb. 22, 1979.

Regarding the much publicized dismissal of Bob Abel's group, Brick Price (whose shop built props for the film) felt that Abel was unfairly maligned in the NEW WEST magazine article, and that as far as he was concerned, "Abel wanted to do a good film. Bob was constantly having battles with Magicam and Paramount and ultimately with Doug Trumbull. Trumbull was working for Paramount and as far as I knew, Bob was working with them and they were moving onward. That business about a minute and a half of film being all they (Abel) had is ludicrous because I saw that much the first day of rushes. The first day I started working on the film I saw more than that amount of footage. But the thing was, Paramount would see something they wouldn't like, such as the spacewalk, and want to reshoot."

Yet Douglas Trumbull ultimately had compliments for the way Robert Abel's group conceived the look of the climax of the film. In the March 1980 CINEFEX, Trumbull stated, "There had been some incredibly elaborate storyboards done at Abel's for this beautiful transformation thing, which was along the lines of a cocoon changing into a butterfly—literally—huge sets of wings folding out and all these other diaphanous things. There were a lot of very nice ideas, but I could never get a handle on exactly how to do it, particularly in the amount of time we had left."

The shot began with live action on a soundstage with the actors facing each other. Powerful Xenon aircraft landing lights shined on them from behind to generate the effect of being surrounded by light. The live action footage was then overlaid with moiré patterns by shooting flat artwork on an animation stand and superimposing it over the live action images.

This was followed by the bursting effect as V'ger supposedly was transformed into another state of being. The most impressive element of this show was what looked like a blue shock wave which seemed to symbolize V'ger fading away into another plane of existence. This was achieved by photographing a curved length of wire which rotated in a complete 360 circle during each exposure. The wire circle was made larger with each exposure so that the overlapping images seemed to rotate outwards from a central point. To simultaneously have the effect of a ring of lights rotating outwards, a tiny grain-of-wheat light bulb was mounted on a black pylon which was rotated in forty-eight different positions around the circle for each frame. This too was done in an expanding manner so that the multiple passes which look like the ring of lights were expanding from a central point.

READY WILLING AND ABEL

Another part of the effect involved shooting a back-lit light source on an animation stand. The light source flickered and had different exposures. This all combined to create the central glow which was at the source of the V'ger explosion from which the Enterprise seemed to be emerging.

While no optical effects by Robert Abel's company made it into the film, some of his live action special effects did. One of these is the glowing V'ger probe which appears on the bridge. Mike Minor, who worked as an illustrator a pseudo assistant art director on the film, described how that footage was accomplished.

"A man wore a black suit and walked about doing it. You'll notice that to wipe him out of the shot they had to do a split—a left and right split. You might notice that one side of the bridge does not quite match up to its counterpart on the right side of the screen. This happened because they were joining two images to wipe the operator and the six foot tubular device out. That was something they rigged—forty thousand volts on that step generator. They blew the power transformers at Paramount and had to bring in a special truck generator just to run that device. Tremendous amount of voltage; a scary device. The device was shot by them (Bob

Abel's company) and the effects material was turned over eventually to either Dykstra or Trumbull."

When it came time to shoot STAR TREK II—THE WRATH OF KHAN, it was discovered that the bridge of the Enterprise was in one piece. This made it difficult for the camera to move in and around the bridge. The Director of Photography on ST—TMP, Richard H. Kline, requested that the bridge be assembled in this manner. Kline didn't like moving walls and preferred working in a closed set. He believed that there was something "unnatural" about moving walls and felt that when walls are taken out, credibility is lost. Kline felt that the actors reacted more like they were in a real setting if the walls were all solidly in place. He admitted, though, that this decision limited the camera angles available to him. To deal with that problem Kline had a monorail installed in the ceiling from which a camera could be suspended.

SECRETS OF THE TRADE

The sonic shower effect was created on-set by Kline using a double beam-splitting device and 3M projection material which is invisible until light strikes it. One of the beam splitters was used to reflect the light waves onto the plastic shower compartment. The wave motion was generated by a tray of water reflecting into mirrors positioned above it. The second beam splitter was used to add the 3M material. The illusion of Ilia's nudity was accomplished by using a light which matched the skin tone of the actress. Then, by using shutters and dimmers, the flesh-colored light was dimmed and a silver light was engaged. When the 3M material was hit by the silver light, Ilia appeared to be wearing a silver costume.

Douglas Trumbull's Entertainment Effects Group shot the special effects in 70mm (although the negative size of the film is 65mm). Other special effects houses sometimes operate differently. Industrial Light & Magic for instance, works in 35mm or 35mm VistaVision.

Once Trumbull took over, many people were brought in to work on miniatures and effects. Trumbull reassembled his entire team from CLOSE ENCOUNTERS, including model-building expert Greg Jein who had supervised the building of the Mothership in that film. Trumbull even moved back into the Glencoe facility on Marina del Rey where his crew had worked on CE3K. That facility housed room for administrative offices, three optical printers, optical line-up facilities, a matte stand and matte painting rooms, editorial facilities, a 65mm black-and-white processor for test shots with room left over for complete wood and machine shops.

There was even one room which could serve as a sound stage for shooting miniatures. The model for the interior shots of V'ger was built here. It was so large that after it was photographed, it was torn apart in order to get it out of the building. A motion control system was built there so that shots of models could be repeated with pinpoint accuracy.

However, due to the demands of ST—TMP, this shop alone wasn't large enough for Trumbull's immediate crew. A second building was leased two blocks away where five more shooting stages were assembled. Another building was used to house the art department and rotoscope equipment, as well as provide workrooms for the designers, illustrators, and animation staff. In the final nine months of the film's production, Trumbull and the units he supervised completed nearly five hundred special effects cuts.

THE KLINGON SHIPS

One of Apogee's major contributions was creating the opening scenes of the Klingon ships. It was John Dykstra who came up with the unusual and effective shot of the Klingon ships headed towards the camera. The camera tilts to look straight down at the ships and then does a roll tilting up again to show the ships going in the opposite direction into the V'ger cloud. It's probably the fanciest camerawork ever seen in a Robert Wise film and led some to expect something more dramatic and creative from the photography throughout the picture.

Only one Klingon ship model was constructed but it was photographed three times and composited to create the image of three different ships. The effect of the photo torpedoes which the Klingons fired was created by reflecting a laser off of a revolving crystal. This was done for both the Klingon ships and the Enterprise, with only the color being changed (red for the Klingon torpedoes, blue for the Enterprise's).

Regarding what was involved in that sequence, Dykstra told AMERICAN CINEMATOGRAPHER, "Doug and I worked on this sequence with the attitude: 'We've got to give the people a really exciting visual experience here—as exciting as we can within the context of telling the story.' So we just set about doing it, but the choreography of that opening sequence was based on a cloud which was not completed until two weeks before the end of production. So there were Klingon warships moving around in space with no cloud to go with them.

We got a model of the Klingon ship and looked at it to see what we could do with the bloody thing. We figured out some moves and storyboarded them and went over them with Bob Wise to see if he would go for them or not. We had to go over them with Doug as well because Doug, at that time, had the intention of generating the cloud in a way that was different from how it was finally generated. We provided moves that were very slow and deliberate, because Bob wanted to preserve a mass look in terms of the ships.

Because of the way the cloud was to be generated, you couldn't move the ships very radically. It was shot using a conventional system—blue screen with one model. The cloud was shot with stars, which made it a composite element when it went into the optical printer to be put together with the other elements. All of the ships were separations. Some of them were run with cover mattes, and some without, depending on how many passes there were. It was kind of tough trying to get the stars to hold up in some of them."

NEW WAYS TO BLOW THINGS UP

Dykstra's crew also had to show the destruction of the three Klingon ships in the opening scenes of the movie. Originally Dykstra was just going to fall back on the tried-and-true methods employed in STAR WARS where models were simply blown up by building fragile versions of the models which had been filmed for other scenes. Trumbull wanted to go a different

~~oute. Since V'ger was actually turning the things it overwhelms into electronically stored in~~ formation, it was decided to go for an image in which an effect strikes a ship and then sweeps over it until it seems to just vanish. This was done late in the production when principal photography was actually completed.

The beam fired by V'ger was achieved by using a xenon bulb. The bulb created a lens flare, which was composited with electric arcs created on a Tesla coil (which emits streaks of electricity from a central position). The effect for the disintegration of the Klingon ships involved wrapping the model with aluminum foil and then reflecting laser light off it. By compositing this effect with a shot of the model, it creates a shimmering effect thus achieving the look of a beam sweeping over the model. The lightning bolt effects were added using animation to complete the effect.

The Klingon ship model was built by Magicam before Dykstra came onto the picture and changes had to be made to it. "That model, when it came to us, had been set up for some other photographic technique that didn't fit with ours. We had to go in and completely redo the lighting. That was done by Grant McCune and the people he had working with him, which is basically a very similar staff to the ones we had on STAR WARS and other shows. They did an incredible job.

They took all the teeny little lights out of the model and put in some lights of significant size—and they did it in a matter of a few days. They really did a nice job of redoing the model, without destroying what was already there. They had to add a lot of detail to it because we got much closer to the model than I think they ever intended to before. Once the thing with the ship was worked out, Doug Smith, in charge of shooting that sequence, photographed the opening shot. We had to shoot double-pass mattes on that, rather than shooting it against a blue screen and it was sort of fun mixing the techniques together."

Trumbull convinced the production designers to build a Klingon bridge resembling the cramped confines of an old submarine. This was designed by Andrew Probert while the set was constructed under the supervision of John Vallone. This Klingon bridge set was constructed in a complicated manner to make optimum use of the special effects techniques they had available to them.

UNIQUE LIVE ACTION FILMING

The set was constructed with six levels of depth. As the ship was being assimilated by V'ger, one level at a time, beginning with the furthest one back, was removed and replaced with a blew screen. This way the digitization effect would seem to be sweeping towards the camera a section at a time. The blue screen which replaced the sections of set allowed the disintegration effects to be added later.

This is an example of live action footage done specifically with the special effects in mind which would be added in post-production. Sequenced light sources were concealed behind each section of the set to tie in with the later special effects. There was a flash of light as each level is absorbed which would merge with the effects added later via bluescreen until the last level was the Klingons themselves turning to witness the effect which sweeps over and engulfs them. On screen it happens quite quickly.

In the February 1980 issue of AMERICAN CINEMATOGRAPHER, John Dykstra explained his facility's approach to doing some of the special effects. "Well, we did some of the Transporter stuff, and the Transporters were basically the same kinds of devices as in the TV show. But this worked quite well actually because if we had changed a lot of it around from what it was like in the TV version and gotten too fancy with it, we would probably have lost a lot of the loyal audience.

Many of those people actually came to see the same kinds of things happening again. At any rate, we added a little laser effect to the outside of the tube and a little bit different kind of sparkle inside it, and then—to dramatize the malfunction—we used a pellicle or mylar mirror distortion to misshape the people who were supposed to be inside the tubes."

Trumbull had Jein's crew working on the Spock spacewalk. Since that was part of the V'ger interior, he had them build larger additional miniatures. Since time was of the essence, they decided not to use matte paintings or lasers. Instead, they built a large miniature and shot it in a smoke room. This took care of the background. The smoke in the "smoke room" was low-grade diesel fuel which had been vaporized and suspended in mid-air. This provided a natural diffusion of the image and made for a realistic perspective.

GREAT PAINTERS AND FX MEN

It gave it what's known as an "aerial perspective." As Trumbull explained it, "We realized that there is a function in real life that great painters know about that's called 'aerial perspective.' That the air is never perfectly clean. If you want a miniature to look more real, you can artificially create aerial perspective through the use of smoke densities when you photograph. Because we are often shooting miniatures and shooting at f.22 for a five or ten second exposure, the smoke density in the room can be controlled to simulate real time. One of the processes we use all the time is the smoke room, and we now have an electronically controlled smoke density that automatically controls the smoke in the room which is completely blacked out and the air circulated. It can accurately control smoke densities for long periods of time."

Since V'ger had often been represented in the film as some sort of cloud, the murky background fit right in with preceding images. This miniature was designed by Syd Mead as well and he came up with elements incorporating a six-sided symmetry so that the manufactured model parts would be easy to duplicate. While Greg Jein and his crew built the bulk of the model, the maw section was assigned to the Maxella shop. There, the orifice was built and motor drives were used to articulate the rhythmic pattern of the opening and closing iris.

Originally the model of the interior of V'ger was built with a massive number of miniature light bulbs. But when these lights didn't photograph in a convincing manner, hundreds of holes were drilled in the model and fiber optics were strung through them. These tiny pinpoints of light gave the model the enormous sense of scale they were after once it was filmed against a smoke background.

The images of the Spock spacewalk were designed by artist Bob McCall, whose astronomical art of NASA is well known. McCall also painted one of the best known movie posters of all time—the image of the Pan Am space clipper exiting the space station for 2001: A SPACE ODYSSEY. McCall's paintings showed the various sights Spock views during his spacewalk inside V'ger.

REALISTIC PAINTINGS

McCall even did a painting of the exterior of V'ger for a view never seen in the film. McCall's paintings for STAR TREK—THE MOTION PICTURE can be found in his book VISION OF THE FUTURE: THE ART OF ROBERT McCALL (Harry N. Abrams, Inc. Publishers, 1982). Not all of the images in McCall's paintings were employed, but some of the most striking ones were, including the image of a giant Ilya floating in space with a glowing orb over her throat. Basically Trumbull used those images from the paintings which he knew his crew could achieve. Trumbull had sketches made based on the paintings and from those sketches Greg Jein's crew built the models.

From those sketches Trumbull assembled a storyboard to tie the images together in a coherent fashion. This changed throughout the filming process as Trumbull had to decide which image preceded what, and at what speed they would be shown. Originally Greg Jein built dozens of Plexiglas planets in different colors and sizes for this sequence. The plan was to align them symmetrically to the right and left sides of the screen. When this proved unworkable, just a few were shot on one side and then flipped and duplicated optically. This way, the right and left sides of the screen were mirror images of each other.

For the scene with the large image of Ilia floating inside V'ger, a plaster cast was made of the head and shoulders of Persis Khambatta and attached to a mannequin. They achieved an interesting effect by finding just the right lighting for the mannequin. These photos were blown up to 16 x 20 prints and retouched. The photos were then shot on an animation stand. The still photo comes across as being a much more complicated effect than it really is.

One of the more interesting touches in the spacewalk sequence are the reflections on the faceplate of Spock's helmet. This was done by mounting an 8mm Nikon fish-eye lens on a 70mm front projection machine. The spacewalk footage was then projected on a three foot Plexiglas dome. The distorted imagery was rephotographed and then superimposed over Spock's faceplate. Both Shatner and Nimoy were brought in to shoot closes for this sequence using a spacesuit rigged with a steel brace so that it wouldn't move and could always be shot at the same specific angles.

A MINIATURE SPOCK

Full figure shots of Spock were done with a two-foot tall miniature which was built by Apogee. The miniature astronaut was made to include remote control articulation on the arms and legs. Once Douglas Trumbull came on as head of the special effects, he abandoned using actors in wire rigs. Instead, he had a full body harness designed to be used by a single stuntman for scenes of someone when they were supposed to be floating in space. The harness fit under the new spacesuit they designed and which was built by Apogee. The spacesuits used prior to Trumbull taking over were jettisoned, which explains why discarded footage cut into the expanded home video edition of ST—TMP doesn't match the new spacesuit used for Spock's spacewalk.

The new spacesuit harness was mounted on a rotating steel post connected to a crane. In this way there was no cumbersome arrangement of wires for the actor to deal with. The stuntman was photographed in front of a blue screen and was used for some of the footage involving the office complex in the orbiting drydock sequence early in the film.

The lightning effects seen during the spacewalk effect were accomplished by generating high-voltage discharges inside containers containing gasses like neon and krypton. This was shot with high speed 35mm and them multiple exposed and optically combined for the final effect.

Some very effective scenes were accomplished in the film using matte paintings. These are paintings which are sometimes done on glass in order to illuminate the image from behind. The scene establishing the setting of San Francisco on Earth at the beginning of the film was shot using a matte. While the Golden Gate bridge seen in the film is a very futuristic version, the 20th century version served as the basis for it. A photo was taken of the modern Golden Gate bridge and then this was flopped left to right to change the perspective.

Matthew Yuricich painted over the old image to change it into some sort of pneumatic conveyance system. Most of the city of San Francisco in the background has been changed to reflect the passage of time, with only the Coit Tower and the Transamerica Building to serve as reference points for 20th century audiences. There is real water on the left side of the bridge but painted water on the right. On the big screen you could see a fish jump in the water as the air tram approaches the tram station.

YOU GOTTA KNOW YOUR MATTES

When Matthew Yuricich first met with the film's director and cinematographer, he came to realize that they didn't know anything about mattes. After describing an aerial shot they wanted him to paint, they wanted to know if the camera could then go around the side of the building. Yuricich had to patiently explain to them that a matte painting is two dimensional, and that if they wanted to take the camera around the side of a building they'd have to build a miniature.

The establishing shot of the tram station as Kirk's tram car arrives is a complicated optical. A floor set was built on a Paramount soundstage with various actors at floor level. There was also a large hanging foreground piece which people in it for scale. The rest of the scene is a matte painting except for the moving air tram which is a model shot added later.

Since the tram had to look like it was in the set, it had to cast a shadow in the wall it was close to, which took some time to perfect to everyone's satisfaction. The tram car in flight was a miniature but as it passed behind columns in the tram station at Star Fleet Headquarters, the transition was made to the full sized model. This had to be done precisely so that the speed of the model matched the speed of the mock-up so that the transition would be seamless.

A painting was used in a different way at the conclusion of the film when the Earth is shown. First Don Moore painted a large illustration of the land and water masses of the Earth. This was then photographed and turned into a large transparency. Clouds were created in a separate photograph by spreading black paper out and dropping talcum powder on it to produce realistic looking cloud shapes.

This was photo-enlarged and airbrushed to add further detail. This was turned into a transparency as well. A duplicate transparency of this was turned into a thin density negative so that the clouds would be darker. All three of these transparencies were projected on a white dome which gave the illusion of clouds above the Earth with the shadow of those clouds beneath.

ON SET EFFECTS

Another painting was used to provide the illusion of size and depth in the engine room set. But instead of a matte, this painting was done on the set as a backdrop to create the perspective right there on the set. On the bottom floor of the set, a perspective painting was laid down to provide the illusion of additional stories. Plus, the area beyond the foreground was squeezed using a forced perspective painting as well as using dwarfs and children in uniforms in the background.

The engine room reactor core is one of the more interesting on-set effects. This was accomplished by using thirty-five light guns, each of which was a self-contained kinetic light projector capable of speed, color changing and light intensity. They were all aligned on a narrow backbone and lowered into the thirty foot tall reactor. Cylindrical rear projection screens were hung in the reactor's interior. The only problem was that at high temperatures the screens tended to melt in reaction to the intense lights, so the amount of time they could be lit for filming was limited. The technicians responsible for coming up with this lighting arrangement were Brian Longbotham and Sam Nicholson. They were also used to light the huge V'ger set where the finale of the film takes place.

Four hundred miles of wiring was used in lighting the massive V'ger set. The set itself was designed to act as a huge light projection surface. To accomplish this, the floor of the set was comprised of thousands of rear-projection panels which were lit from below. The set was constructed seven feet above the floor since most of the lighting systems was placed beneath it. The nine translucent towers around the perimeter of the set were illuminated by one thousand watt quartz nook lights in each of the towers.

Whenever V'ger was supposed to be agitated, the lighting effect was achieved by using thirty one thousand watt xenon arc lights to project light onto various screens around the set. The lights required three thousand AC amps plus two thousand DC amps. In order to keep from burning out transformers and generators, the multiple effects had to be carefully choreographed and in sync due to the massive amount of power they used.

Originally Douglas Trumbull was thinking about using a lot of laser effects in the film. Ultimately he decided to use them only on the wormhole sequence. In order to generate the tunnel pattern of the laser waves, an audio synthesizer was used. It could create exact circular patterns and by fluctuating them slightly with potentiometers, they could suggest movement as they shot them on film, frame by frame. The laser beam was controlled by a computer which was linked up to the camera. The camera used a wide lens and operated on a twenty foot track which allowed it to move back and forth relative to a two-foot rear projection screen.

A VERY COMPLICATED SEQUENCE

Because the laser was turquoise, that's what color the wormhole footage originally was. Since Trumbull didn't want it to be that color, the footage was turned into a black and white low-contrast copy which was used with a color filter to render the final orange-brown color.

The special effects of the wormhole as it looked from inside the Enterprise was actually the only footage completely finished by Bob Abel's crew. It was a complicated sequence which took seven months to add all the streaking effects. Each streak involved a separate pass of the camera and involved projecting the live action footage on a rear projection screen and masking out those sections which they wanted to streak. For the most part this was faces and lights. Even after the streaking footage was completed, it all had to be superimposed on the live action footage used in the movie.

In order to shoot the many complicated elements which made up the V'ger images, a multi-plane photography system was used. This was done using multiple exposures on the same piece of film where different portions of the film are exposed each time. For instance, the first exposure would be two feet from the camera while the second exposure would be four feet and on and on to create an illusion of depth on the film. By photographing them on the same piece of film, they seem to flow together seamlessly into a single image or scene. This was used principally in the V'ger cloud effects as well as in the warp drive sequences. The version of warp drive shown in ST—TMP has become the standard which has been followed in all versions of STAR TREK ever since.

Trumbull's involvement even extended to work directly involving the live action photography. Trumbull stated in the March 1980 issue of CINEFEX magazine, "The Spock space-walk, for example, is a total one hundred percent change from the sequence that was designed, built and photographed under Abel's supervision. Both versions start out the same—the Enterprise is stuck inside V'ger and no one knows what's going on; so Spock commandeers a spacesuit and goes outside to snoop around. In the original, however, when Kirk discovers Spock's out there, he gets in a spacesuit and goes after him—in the process of which he's caught up in a mass of sensor-type organisms and nearly killed. Of course, Spock comes back and saves the day and the two of them continue on together through several different chambers in the V'ger ship."

BORING, BORING, BORING

Trumbull believed that what had originally been scripted was much more interesting. He also thought that the spacesuit designs were poor. Added to this was the fact that in Abel's version, the optical effects which still needed to be combined with the live action photography would be so extensive that it would require half the special effects budget of the picture to finish the sequence, one which Trumbull regarded as dull and overlong.

"We had a screening of the rough cut and when it came to the spacewalk the whole movie just fell apart. What they'd done was produce a very literalized and simplistic version of a concept which in the script was really kind of mind boggling. In spite of the fact that they'd already spent a million dollars on the sequence, it was apparent to me that it was going to cost about half of our total special effects budget and most of our resources just to save it with matte paintings and opticals and make the effects work somewhat as designed. But even at best I never thought it was going to net a very exciting result because the whole concept was just boring.

"So it was my recommendation," Trumbull continued, "to scrap the whole sequence and start over. With all the money and effort they'd already expended, it took a bit of doing to convince everyone that it should be abandoned outright; but once everybody agreed that we should take another shot at it, I sat down and wrote a new spacewalk sequence based on some ideas I wanted to try which I felt we could do in the time we had. Basically, it was my intent to try and find a way to put some of the magic back in and turn it into a dynamic, exciting sequence that would blitz by in two or three minutes and be over with so the story could carry on. I decided not to involve Kirk at all and just redesign it as a personal thing for Spock—a high-speed psychedelic trip through the stored images and memories of everything V'ger had encountered during its journey."

Pieces of the discarded sequence involving Kirk exists in the current version of STAR TREK—THE MOTION PICTURE, available on home video. The unfinished nature of this footage is apparent when Kirk descends from the Enterprise and the wooden rafters in the roof of the soundstage are clearly visible. This is raw footage wherein the visible parts of the soundstage would have been covered with matte paintings had the sequence not been abandoned. These scenes were not supposed to be included in the home video and are an embarrassing oversight.

SPARKLETTS IN SPACE

The spacesuits originally designed for the film had helmets which looked like Sparkletts water bottles. Brick Price worked on ST—TMP providing many of the props used in the production, although his name was inadvertently left off the credits. Regarding the spacesuits, Price stated, "We had originally designed the spacesuit for air conditioning so you wouldn't have a problem with fog on the faceplate, and also for the comfort of the actors. We found some material that would have been wonderful, but they ended up using this pudgy stuff which was real hot and sweaty. At one point I walked into the sound stage into what they called the trench sequence, which they ultimately abandoned.

Price added, "It had awful looking plastic pyramids in it and when I walked around the corner to view the angle of the camera, nobody was there. I thought at first that someone was fooling around because they had a dummy in a suit hanging up there and it looked like someone had been hung. Suddenly I realized and shouted, 'Oh My God! You're killing Spock!' They took him down and it turned out that Nimoy had passed out from the carbon dioxide collecting in his suit. The heat had built up and become unbearable. There are wires that came up through the crotch which could strangle you around the waist and it's unbearable inside a wetsuit and helmet."

The new spacewalk sequence with Spock required Nimoy to return to shoot additional scenes. This was apparently done in July as Roddenberry remarked on August 2, 1979 that principal photography (filming with the actors) had just been completed.

Greg Jein and his crew weren't hired on to build the models for this new sequence until a month later, around the sixth of September. Bear in mind that ST—TMP was slated for release December 7th. "Our involvement originally was just doing the elements for Spock's space walk. For instance, the planets, the inner surfaces, the V'ger moon, V'ger egg and 'lips in space' as we call them. Then about three or four weeks into the production, Doug (Trumbull) called me over to his office and said, 'We've got one more miniature to build and its got no real designs on it. It's the interior of V'ger and it's kind of important to the film, so you guys better swing on that.' So we just started working on it using some blueprints by Syd Mead. I had to build a miniature from the drawings so I could visualize how we were going to build it."

RUSH TO THE FINISH

Since Greg Jein and his crew didn't start work until three months before the release date of the movie, their schedule was unusually hectic. "Usually on a show," Greg explained, "the company is concerned about the money being spent and the material, labor and things like that. But in this case, Paramount just said, 'Do it. Work hundreds of hours a week,' which we did! For a couple weeks we worked a hundred hours a week; sometimes we never left, just stayed three days straight. They just wanted it done for the show. As it was progressing it sort of 'growed,' "Jein stated, using the made up word they'd applied to the situation during the course of production. "More and more lighting was used to make it look better; we wound up using 23 miles of Fibre Optics.

"We were constantly being visited by production people from Paramount saying, 'Could you do it a little faster? Don't go out for dinner; we'll bring it to you.' I don't remember exactly, but we were about three days over the deadline, and we were the first ones to get our section done. Other sections came along about a week later. So they were sort of ticked off at us at first, but as things progressed they lightened up on us. It was very close. I'm almost positive we were shooting up to three weeks before the release date."

John Dykstra also discussed the pressures and long hours spent working on the film when he stated in the February 1980 AMERICAN CINEMATOGRAPHER, "Let's put it this way: frankly, the whole thing was a life or death struggle for all of those people. It was a total group effort, because I wouldn't have had enough energy—even if I'd had all the money and all the people in the world—to get all that stuff done. Nobody could direct everything that had to be ready right down to the minute without having crews who were capable of coming in and giving 110 percent of themselves to the project. They did it over a period of three months—12 to 18 hours a day, seven days a week. They truly got into it. There were casualties, of course; some people got sick. It's hard enough to generate that kind of enthusiasm for a picture even if you started on it from scratch, but to have people come in halfway through and get that hot for it is amazing. Beyond the crew, the technology itself is sort of miraculous."

The model of the interior of V'ger was built by Greg Jein's crew in two sections split vertically, each being about ten feet long. The maw was built by Russ Simpson's crew. But that encompassed only two-thirds of the original design. Another twelve foot section was begun but they realized that it wouldn't fit in the smoke room. Work on that was stopped and the material was discarded before it was ever made available for shooting. The missing section was a hexagonal corridor which would have contained many elongated teardrops. Regarding what happened to the V'ger models after they were filmed, Jein revealed, "They were chain-sawed—at least all of V'ger was. The smaller pieces like the space lips and the egg [From Spock's space walk] are stored somewhere. But most of the smaller planets and things are gone; we gave them away to anyone who came in."

A NEVER ENDING PROCESS

Even after Jein's unit has completed a model, the process doesn't always end there. They have to hope that the people photographing it know what they're doing or else problems can result. "The camera placement and movements are all done by the Director of Photography. I don't touch the camera at all because I'm not in that union. The lighting is all handled by the electricians and the grips. I don't do any of that. We tend to use people who know how the models are made so they know how to, say, put the light here or light it this way, or else we might get a guy who'd just walk over the set and step on everything and break it. That's happened before."

Even after the optical chores were expanded and farmed out to a number of facilities, there was infighting. This made it very difficult for the companies to work together. Brick Price Movie Miniatures discovered this when they visited Magicam. "Magicam wanted to do everything with the effects and miniatures themselves, even though they were overloaded and understaffed," Brick Price recalled. "One day we went down there to collaborate on something because we were all working on the same film. When I got there and was introduced, they literally slammed the door in my face! As far as I know, we and all the other groups got along extremely well."

Brick Price wasn't the only one who reported problems with Magicam. In the March 1980 issue of FANTASTIC FILMS, Andrew Probert, who designed many of the major models in the film, including the new versions of the Enterprise and the Klingon ship, reported an altercation.

"Yes, well, I did have a rather interesting first encounter with Magicam. When I first visited their shop and saw a partially built Klingon cruiser, it was apparent to me that its neckpiece was crooked. As part of my newly assigned responsibilities, I brought this to their attention. The design of the cruiser, with its varying proportions and angles, was such that no one else had noticed it and when I came out of the blue with my observation it didn't go over too well. They told me that it would cost too much time and money to correct. As it turned out, at a much later time in the production, the need arose for a structural change, so the neck was realigned at that time. From that time forward, nothing in the way of design or drawing submitted by me was ever acceptable to Magicam."

A NEW ENTERPRISE

Magicam was a Paramount subsidiary. The footage they generated included the Enterprise in drydock, the Vulcan shuttle and all the travel pods and work bees in the drydock sequence. Although miniatures were used of the Enterprise in drydock (or spacedock) for some scenes, in others the drydock was matted over the Enterprise. This was to obtain a more adequate depth of field in the images than could be managed using the miniatures.

Although Trumbull had his own model-makers working on various aspects of the film, Magicam built the new version of the Enterprise, under the supervision of Jim Dow. The new Enterprise was designed by Andrew Probert, based on a design Joe Jennings had done for the STAR TREK II television series. The Enterprise itself was built around an aluminum armature which was machined at Magicam by Lee Ettleman. The armature was constructed of high strength aluminum to make the model rigid and insure that it didn't flex at any of the key pressure points.

It had to be so strong that the model could support itself even if it was mounted at an angle to be photographed. Once the armature was strong enough, the shell was added and the lights installed. Since it was intended that the saucer portion would not be opened again, neon tubing was installed there for the lights. This was safe because neon lasts thousands of hours and generates very low levels of heat. It was decided to seal the saucer section because stresses on the model would be such that were it ever opened, it would be nearly impossible to seal up again.

The saucer section was made from vacuformed AVS plastic and was four feet in diameter. The Enterprise model also included in its construction Plexiglas, styrene and some wood used on the interior to help form the shape of the hull. A variety of adhesives were used in assembling the model.

The seven foot Enterprise which Magicam built turned out to be smaller than it should have been. A miscalculation was made and Magicam was told to build a model which turned out to be difficult to photograph. At seven feet in length, the Enterprise lacked the kind of detail necessary for good close-ups and "beauty" shots. For example, to obtain the look achieved in previous science fiction films, the Discovery in 2001: A SPACE ODYSSEY had been fifty-four feet long, while in SILENT RUNNING the spacecraft was twenty-six feet long.

The Enterprise model was also quite heavy. The special effects crew at Industrial Light & Magic often complained how difficult the model was to work with. Also, the Enterprise model's surface had to be repainted after ST—TMP. The model was originally detailed so that its surface appeared to be comprised of hundreds of individual panels, each with their own refraction. However, reflections caused "holes" to appear in the model when filmed so the skin was repainted to make it dull and give it a non-reflective surface.

LET THERE BE LIGHT

Trumbull's team didn't seem to have any trouble lighting and filming the Enterprise for ST—TMP. For the space dock scene, the dry dock was hung from the ceiling while the Enterprise was supported by a post on the floor. A computer kept track of the position of the various other miniatures used in the space dock sequence for purposes of matting in the star field background. The lighting in this and other scenes involving the miniatures was very important in order to create the illusion that these weren't miniatures.

While the space dock and the Enterprise were constructed with internal lighting, Trumbull's crew added additional lighting when they filmed them. For instance, the spotlights which shine down on the Enterprise as it's preparing to disembark were positioned through the use of dental mirrors to reflect the lights in order to create a spotlight effect.

Trumbull tends to avoid using the bluescreen process which ILM prefers. Trumbull feels that while bluescreen is fine for hard-edged mattes, it doesn't give him the clarity he wants to see in the optical effects he shoots. Trumbull prefers working in 70mm and with motion control. They use a second pass of the camera to pull mattes off and thereby create a contrast matte which is painted black. A matte is a black and white silhouette image on a piece of film. It's usually a high contrast film image used in an optical printer for the purpose of superimposing images together.

Then there's the matte stand, another important element in special effects photography. The matte stand is used with matte paintings. Matte paintings are usually done on glass and the matte stand allows the technicians to film them in focus, front-lit and back-lit. Planes of glass can be etched for opaque mattes, positive or negative mattes or other kinds required by whatever lighting they want to use in a scene.

For ST—TMP, most of the mattes and miniatures were back-lit. Other effects shops photograph a model while it is front-lit and then a matte is filmed while the model is back-lit to obtain a high contrast image. By shooting a model back-lit, there is no light falling on the model itself—it's completely black. They then make a print from the matte, load it into an Oxberry animation camera, and use the camera to project the images of the matte down on the animation table and use the print as a reference. This is a form of rotoscoping to create artwork with which you can draw a line which will stay outside the miniature. This is then combined with a negative of the matte to block out all the unwanted areas. The unwanted areas exist because the miniature is filmed against a background which is only just slightly larger than the model itself.

"GARBAGE MATTES"

In the drydock scene, the first matte shot of the Enterprise with the unwanted elements in it is called the "garbage matte." The unwanted elements are subsequently removed to make a clean matte. Where there are two backgrounds, a transparency of artwork is projected into white film with the stars arranged to avoid the part of the image where the Earth will be located. For the scene showing the planet Vulcan, three plates were used to create the matte which formed Vulcan. One plate was the matte painting, which was painted on glass. The second was a smoke element. The third plate contained the live action elements. The smoke elements were arranged so that when superimposed they seemed to emanate from the volcanoes in the scene showing the surface of Vulcan.

Motion control is a system whereby movements of the camera, or even a miniature, are recorded in a computer so that the special effects technicians can repeat those exact movements with pinpoint accuracy. Any kind of dynamic physical motion can be controlled by motion control systems. While motion control seems to have come into being in the late seventies, it was actually used in a less refined way (without computers) on 2001: A SPACE ODYSSEY in the mid-sixties.

Trumbull's method of photographing miniatures involves the camera panning rather than having the models move. The mattes can then be applied on the same piece of film to create a composite, which keeps the background from double-exposing through the miniatures.

Regarding the trials of shooting the various models used in ST—TMP, Trumbull's model shop sometimes found it necessary to add detailing when it came time to shoot certain scenes. When the Travel Pod docks, an enlarged section of the office complex was built to shoot the kind of detail which was unobtainable on the smaller version of that model.

The Travel Pod, in which Kirk and Scotty travel over to the Enterprise while it's in drydock, involved shooting live-action footage on a stage against black velvet and then having that footage rear-projected into the Travel Pod. This is one of those cases where the grain in the film is apparent as the live action footage seemed to have been shot on 35mm so that when it was rear-projected into the Travel Pod for the scene when it was shot, we're seeing a second generation of the footage by the time it is projected on the theatre screen.

CREATIVE JUICES FLOW

V'ger was an element of the picture which underwent a lot of changes. Since the script wasn't very specific on this aspect of the story, it was left wide open for the boundaries of the production designer's imagination to try to capture. Robert Abel's team came up with something cigar-shaped which had strange surface details and ultimately looked like some sort of fish. Originally the maw through which the Enterprise entered V'ger was at one end, like a blimp, and it opened like a clamshell. Douglas Trumbull found that to be a rather boring design element.

When Abel was still in charge of the special effects, and Richard Taylor was the Art Director, Brick Price Movie Miniatures did some work creating a model of V'ger. The model they started on in August of 1978 looked like a cigar with a maw which opened up. They disliked that design because it too much resembled the planet killer in "The Doomsday Machine" television episode. By that time there was already a lot of behind-the-scenes controversy over the screenplay resembling the TV episode "The Changeling."

Said Price, "We did a lot of tests working with textures like paint, color and light, things of that sort, and it wound up with a very organic art-deco look to it. Taylor was an avid deco fan.

That one might have been interesting had they gone with it. It would have had a bubble on it and the Voyager craft would have been on an island underneath one of those. The whole skin surface was sort of iridescent. Paramount decided to have miles and miles of white and not let people know what it looked like exactly. Ours was really bizarre and all convoluted with things hanging off it. So every time it changed hands it changed completely. Taylor's original concept of V'ger was extremely complex. You can see all sorts of actual light functions and all sorts of spheres representing the V'ger concept of life."

The final drawings of V'ger which were done by Syd Mead were executed under the guidance of Douglas Trumbull and John Dykstra. "I was brought in at the tail end," Mead recalls. "They'd already done all the live shooting, but on post-production and special effects they were up against a very tight time schedule. Both Doug Trumbull's facility and John Dykstra's company, Apogee, were working 24 hours a day for months before the film came out and I understand that they actually shipped some second generation prints for projection because they didn't have time to make enough first generation prints to meet the release date.

TEAM EFFORT

"When I came on the film, at the request of John Dykstra, they had already hired a mathematics computer professor who designed the cam-operated mouth of V'ger. I gave it a few twists so where the six sides would come together you'd have an apex, and I did things along each of those apexes. That meant that we only had to build one side of the hexagonal solid, in effect, which was the camera track down the length of this forty-seven foot model [of V'ger] and because the ridges sort of came up on each side you could get away with that. Originally they were going to film the entire object as a six-sided solid, but we just took the other way out as a time saving device.

Mead continued, "The screenwriters can write something like: It's something that no man has ever seen before—now go ahead and do that. So Robert Wise cut out little script paragraphs to impress on us the fact that we had to do this. He didn't want old bridges. He didn't want mechanical looking fixture detail. What we had to come up with was a mechanical-organic kind of look to the thing with depth to it as it was layered and had grown layers so that the real energy was down inside.

He goes on, "What they had done was taken a camera track and made it into a three-dimensional object to favor the camera track because they first approach V'ger from what is actually its rear end and they travel the whole length of the object to the mouth in the front. They then turn around and go inside and essentially go halfway through the chamber where the final, almost magic, process takes place. They were doing some strange configurations as we had to keep that camera track and that's why I decided to make it into a tube, for all practical purposes, to preserve that whole camera track that they'd already storyboarded. But after this mathematics professor designed the working principle for the maw, then I thought up the decoration for that to make it look like it was a mile across or whatever."

Mead discovered that the apparent scale of the object kept changing, as it often does in movies. "Something could be five miles across in one shot and you'd detail for that scale, and then another object comes into the camera range and violates the scale you've set up, but you get by with it because of the dramatic intent of the scene. It was never really established how big V'ger was. In one conversation in the script they were who knows how far away from it and it was supposed to be seven hundred miles long. Well, I made a diagram, just for my own education, and at that distance with the visual angle they used, it would have been three thousand miles long. So the scale kept changing.

MORE V'GER WORK

"The detail we went after was of an electronic landscape which had solidified into various polarity crystals and directions and that sort of aspect," Mead explained. "It was fascinating painting. So I was the one who designed the surface detail, and then, of course, the model-makers go to work and they follow the concept, but they add in fine detail and the process produces the end result of the model you have."

When asked about the visualization of V'ger, John Dykstra stated, "It was probably a combination of people, but Syd Mead did some illustrations on the show and he turned out to be incredible in his ability to take something that was absolutely intangible in the minds of the people who wrote, directed and produced this film and come up with something that they liked. They had some expansive concepts, but for all of their involvement with the thing in the script, nobody could put a physical shape or direction or look on it. So Syd came up with this V'ger thing, and on top of that he came up with a reason for why it was shaped the way it was and how it worked, which was really great. His illustrations served very, very precisely as a basis for the imagery that ended up in the film."

The miniature of the exterior of V'ger was constructed in several large sections at Apogee. What they were trying to accomplish was to make an organic looking machine, but while it certainly looks quite weird in the movie, whether it looks organic is a matter of conjecture. Since what we see of V'ger looks strange and unlike anything we've ever seen before, it's difficult to state that it looks organic.

Since Trumbull was unhappy with previous designs of the V'ger maw, the opening through which the Enterprise enters the massive machine intelligence, he hired Ron Resch to design it. Resch is a well-known designer of foldable space-frame systems. He came up with a series of six double-ended cones which were faceted and interlocked with a hexagonal orifice. It was so complicated that a model of it had to be built in order for Resch to demonstrate his design. Unfortunately, in the film the complexities of this design are largely lost in the two-dimensional medium of the motion picture.

In spite of the time crunch, things were tried which ultimately were discarded from the film. Mike Minor described one such sequence. "For instance, when they did the wing-walk on the hull of the ship, we had blacked out a whole stage and set up the hexagonal cubes that they step off of the ship and walk across to V'ger's brain section. We had originally planned to have the cubes light up. Now you can get scuttled as a designer by your cameraman, and this cameraman, Richard Kline, didn't like the look; was afraid of it. I think his gaffer and he were afraid to try to light it. The cubes were supposed to light up as they walked on them. It could have been a great look. There was a wonderful fluttering glow in all of them.

ALWAYS A RUSH

"We did a test, it looked fine," Minor continued, "but inexplicably they wound up being painted grey so you had this cold, dull look. I had built a number of pieces which hung as 'chandelier' units which were revealed by electric bursts within them and then they winked out and you couldn't see them. These were hung out in front of the ship and they were to be on and off as forms that were lit by electrical bursts in the void. Then they disappear and leave electrical energy about them for a moment.

Minor goes on, "We were rushing to get the thing done and they were built mechanically. They worked on that stuff for a month with me designing and them executing in Plexiglas, opaque materials, back-lighting them, wiring the thing and L.E.D.'s. I remember them being hung there and Trumbull and I standing there with our arms folded, looking up, and I looked over and said, 'Well, do you think they're going to make it into the picture?' and he just shook his head and said, 'No.' But they let us go ahead and play with them just the same."

John Dykstra's company, Apogee, became a major subcontractor on ST—TMP, ultimately becoming responsible for thirty percent of the special effects. The opening sequence of the film, involving the three Klingon cruisers and the Epsilon 9 space station which all become victims of V'ger, were among some of Apogee's more impressive effects. Even though Douglas Trumbull was technically supervising all of the special visual effects, Apogee worked more closely with director Robert Wise. Trumbull correctly believed that since Dykstra and his crew had managed to produce the effects for STAR WARS by themselves, that it wasn't necessary to be looking over their shoulder.

While the live action footage on STAR TREK—THE MOTION PICTURE was shot on 35mm film, the optical effects were shot on 65mm. This is because when shooting special effects on film, elements are often combined which requires duplicating the film. Every time a dupe, is made the quality of the picture is reduced. By starting with a larger image in 65mm, when it is combined with other elements and reduced to 35mm, the clarity of the picture is comparable with the footage originally shot on 35mm.

Since John Dykstra had come up with a striking interpretation of the opening scene of the movie, Douglas Trumbull wanted to come up with something equally interesting for the conclusion. What he came up with was the Enterprise moving past the camera and entering warp. [We're not supposed to consider the fact that the ship enters warp while in orbit around the Earth.]

THE BIG PREMIER

At last, STAR TREK—THE MOTION PICTURE appeared in theaters on December 7, 1979. Anticipation was great; rumors that Kirk and the crew met God still persisted from some years earlier. The story developed from the old "Robot's Return" story treatment had reached its final stage.

The problem with this movie was its slow, ponderous development; its all-too awestruck reverence for its own special effects (which are beautifully done, it must be admitted— but frequently all too static), and most of all for the short shrift it gives to its own characters' relationships with each other. In essence, like Spock in his initial appearance, the film is too clinical and dispassionate to engage the emotions.

In scenes cut from the theatrical release but restored on video, this is somewhat less the case; each character has his moments. Here, Spock actually weeps after his mind meld with V'ger. Why these scenes were cut remain a mystery. Another restored scene, showing a space suited Kirk emerging from a cargo bay, is notable for the fact that no special effects were ever cued into it; the viewer can see, briefly, the soundstage structure behind him.

Leonard Nimoy had this to say about STAR TREK—THE MOTION PICTURE: "I think we should say, in deference to the people who made the first Star Trek motion picture, that they had a very special set of problems. For example, there had not been a Star Trek project for eleven years. We finished making the series in 1968 and here we were in 1979, coming together to do a different Star Trek project. That meant that a lot of very special circumstances had to be addressed. Ground had to be broken in a special kind of way. Do you make comment in the film that eleven years has passed and therefore things have changed? The ship has changed, the uniform has changed, the sets have changed, rank has changed, relationships have changed. We were faced with the concern that we should not be perceived as a blown-up television episode, but should be looked upon as a motion picture. therefore there were certain changes that were expected by the audience, and they must be addressed."

Production Illustrator Andy Probert, who contributed so much to the look of the vehicles in the film, had this to say about the movie in the March 1980 issue of FANTASTIC FILMS. "Despite all the reported problems that seem to have plagued this movie and the varying degrees of feelings of the crews, good and bad, one can't help but get an incredible sense of satisfaction from seeing vehicles and space structures on film whose designs were originated by myself. I'm optimistic that this movie will be a big turning point in the history of STAR TREK."

THE REAL STORY

Greg Jein seemed to reflect a more commonly held view among the technicians who labored on this epic production. "I wish it could have been a better film. I was disappointed. A lot of us were. I would've liked to have seen them put a lot of the stuff back in that they took out. There were a lot of things that were conceptualized, but the time wasn't there to do them. Bob McCall painted some really large paintings and one of them was of the exterior of V'ger, but they didn't have time to pull it off."

Supposedly, director Robert Wise was unhappy with the final cut of the film; Paramount vetoed any re-editing in order to make the all-important release date. People who attended the Washington, D.C. premiere of the feature reported observing Wise burying his face in his hands at various points in the film, obviously embarrassed.

Although the video release provides the opportunity to see STAR TREK—THE MOTION PICTURE at its best, the film remains a fairly disappointing first contact with the big screen as far as the entire STAR TREK mythos is concerned. Yet right to the very end, Gene Roddenberry maintained that this was still the best of the STAR TREK motion pictures.

SPECIAL EFFECTS

PHOTO GALLERY

Close-up of the original 18-foot model of the Enterprise from the classic 1960s television series.

Completed special effect shot of the original Enterprise from the episode "The Tholian Web".

Complete special effects shot for "Space Seed".

PHOTO GALLERY

PHOTO GALLERY

Close-up of the original Romulan ship model used in "Balance of Terror".

PHOTO GALLERY

From "The Doomsday Machine". This is an actual AMT model kit used to create a cheap special effect. Note the number on the ship is achieved by transposing the digits of the original Enterprise decal number 1701 into 1017.

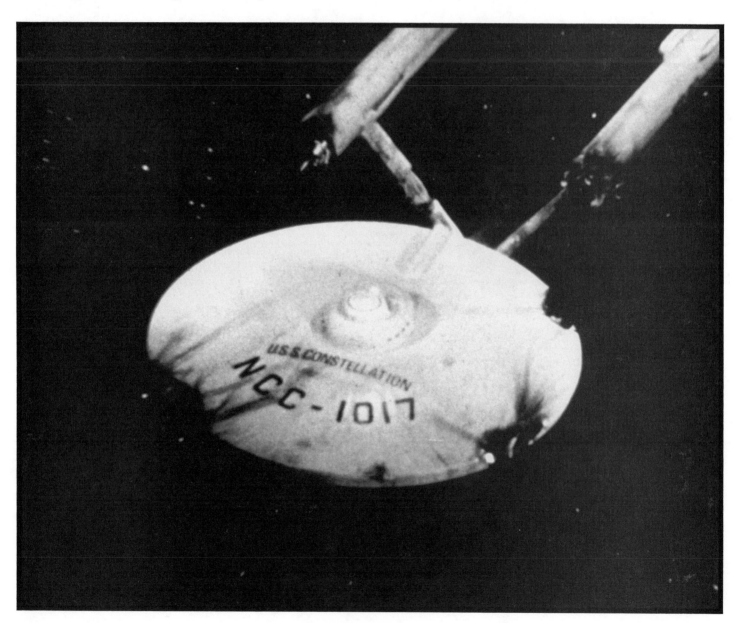

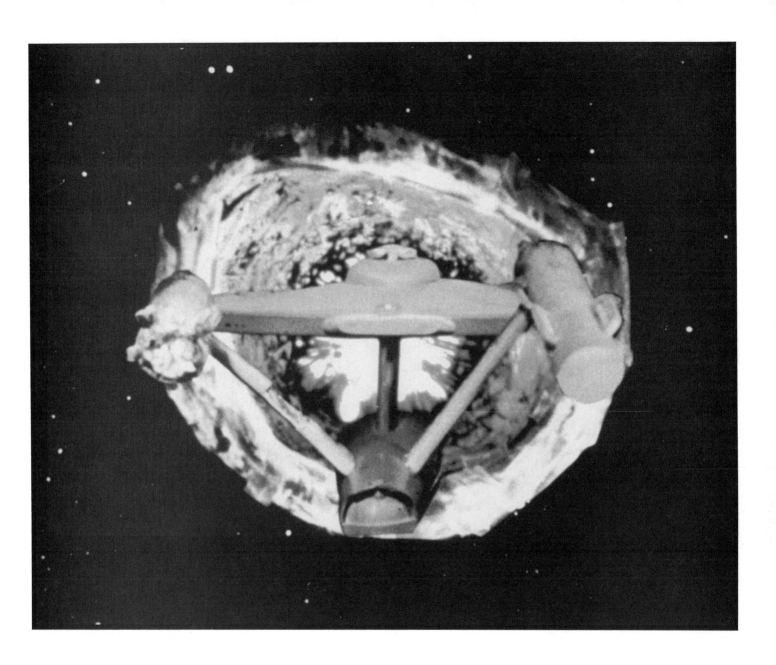

The AMT model kit used in "The Doomsday Machine". In the episode, the fragile model wiggles in some close-ups.

PHOTO GALLERY

The original Klingon ship seen in "The Enteprise Incident". Only one model was built as the other two in the scene were added optically.

PHOTO GALLERY

PHOTO GALLERY

The original Enterprise with the phasers added as a special effect.

PHOTO GALLERY

From STAR TREK: THE MOTION PICTURE, the new Enterprise under attack from V'Ger.

The new Enterprise—supposedly a revised version of the old Enterprise. This ship began the trend of tinkering with the Enterprise in the first few movies, ultimately leading to a new Enterprise for THE NEXT GENERATION.

PHOTO GALLERY

A full year went by after the release of STAR TREK—THE MOTION PICTURE before it was decided to produce a sequel. This time, Paramount was determined not to be sunk with an enormous special effects budget.

3

The Wrath of Khan

In 1982, STAR TREK II: THE WRATH OF KHAN redressed the failing of the previous STAR TREK motion picture. Unlike its predecessor, it contained a strong engaging plot, plenty of action, a powerful nemesis, dramatic relationships and special effects used in a more interesting fashion.

Paramount kept tight reigns on the budget. It only cost thirteen million to make, less than a third of the maximum estimates of the first film. On the other hand, it grossed eighty million dollars in its initial domestic release alone. Paramount definitely made a big time profit on STAR TREK II: THE WRATH OF KHAN.

Special effects this time around were provided by Industrial Light and Magic, the effects company that grew out of George Lucas' STAR WARS projects. Director Nicholas Meyer didn't want to go through all of the special effects headaches which ST—TMP did. With Paramount's blessing, they went with what the director called "the Rolls Royce of special effects."

Industrial Light & Magic was actually chosen by producer Robert Sallin. Initially he hired Jim Danforth as a consultant while he was trying to decide who would do the special effects. Although the effects work on ST—TMP was splintered between a number of different outfits, the short schedule they had to do STAR TREK II in made that prohibitive. Sallin decided that he wanted all the effects handled under one roof. He had Jim Danforth break down the special effects into a budget and a schedule so that the producer would have something to refer to and compare with the bids he'd get from the various companies he spoke with. Sallin held extensive meetings with a number of firms, and finally decided on Industrial Light & Magic.

Initially, executive producer Harve Bennett was reluctant to go with ILM because of their location (they're based some three hundred miles north of Los Angeles, in San Rafael near San Francisco). However, Industrial Light & Magic had already proven itself with STAR WARS, THE EMPIRE STRIKES BACK, DRAGONSLAYER and RAIDERS OF THE LOST ARK.

ILM IS BORN

Industrial Light & Magic was born in June 1975 when George Lucas and producer Gary Kurtz were organizing a team to do the special effects work for STAR WARS. John Dykstra was put in charge and assembled a team of craftsmen and technicians. Initially ILM was set up in Van Nuys, California, just outside Los Angeles in a huge storage facility which was divided into departments so that they could produce everything they needed in one locale.

ILM was initially set up to include a model shop, a carpentry shop, a machine shop, an electronics shop, a rotoscope department, an optical printing department and a film control department which coordinated the film elements of the special effects. John Dykstra supervised the design and construction of a special camera which allowed the camera to move on seven different axis of movement and tied it to a computer so that the camera could duplicate complex movements. This camera was initially called the Dykstraflex, but after John Dykstra and George Lucas had a falling out and Dykstra left to form Apogee, the camera just became known as the "flex."

The three-hundred sixty special effects shots created for STAR WARS made it a milestone film and established the technical credibility of everyone who worked on it. After STAR WARS was released and before THE EMPIRE STRIKES BACK went into production, ILM was relocated out of the Los Angeles. George Lucas disliked the pressures of working in such close proximity to the motion picture community day in and day out.

But ILM did not come on board without some behind-the-scenes controversy. Industrial Light & Magic was supposedly chosen by Paramount because it had the winning bid. But Douglas Trumbull, whose Entertainment Effects Group worked on ST—TMP, claimed to have offered a bid which was $1.5 million lower than ILM's. At the time, Paramount refused to comment on this, stating only that Douglas Trumbull had also put a time limitation on his involvement due to his preparations to begin directing the film BRAINSTORM.

Some felt that Paramount chose ILM in order to further their relations with Lucasfilm, whom they were in partnership with on the Indiana Jones films. When STAR TREK II included stock footage of some special effects first used in ST—TMP, Trumbull complained at the time because his involvement with those retread effects was not credited in the motion picture. Trumbull has not worked on any of the subsequent STAR TREK motion pictures.

MIXING OLD WITH NEW

Even though they were able to reuse the Enterprise built for the previous film, some new models had to be built especially for STAR TREK II. The most notable of these is the Reliant, the ship stolen by Khan. The Reliant was designed at Paramount and then turned over to ILM to make. Recognizing the problems with the large, heavy Enterprise model, Steve Gawley, the supervising model maker at ILM, made certain that the Reliant was smaller, lighter and less complex to wire for lighting.

A network of switches on the Enterprise model had to be rewired every time the model was prepared for filming. The Reliant was made of vacu-formed plastic and was light enough that two people could maneuver it into position for filming. It took eight people to manhandle the Enterprise model so that it could be mounted in front of the camera. Other modelmakers who worked on the Reliant were Sean Casey, Mike Fulmer, Brian Chin, Steve Sanders, Martin Brenneis, Jeff Mann, Bill George, Bob Diepenbrock and Larry Tan.

Because Trumbull's outfit filmed the Enterprise with a moving camera, they lit it in peculiar ways which created problems trying to film the model any other way. Certain spotlights on the Enterprise which illuminated the numbers and other markings consisted of tiny lights on the model which were mounted so that they could be reflected off external mirrors and shine back on the model with a spotlight effect. Since it was virtually impossible to have the model roll and have the spotlights roll with it, Ken Ralston had to find ways to move the camera in order to simulate movement of the model. It didn't take him long to come to hate that Enterprise model.

For purposes of long shots, small models of the Reliant and the Enterprise were made. For important close-ups, large sections of the models were built. This way, sections of the ship could be damaged or destroyed without damaging the primary models. For instance, on the Reliant the portion of the model referred to as the "roll bar" is blown up. This portion of the Reliant was filmed in front of a backdrop of the nebula. In order to be able to do the shot more than once, the piece was designed to come apart but remain relatively intact.

IT'S ALL AN ILLUSION

Explosive charges inside the "roll bar" blew out pre-packed pieces of plastic scrap, thereby giving the illusion that the ship was being blown apart. As the pieces from inside the model were jettisoned, it made it look as though more damage was being done than there really was. The part of the model which blew up was constructed of wax, which could easily be remolded for another shot. The addition of opticals of the phaser beam as well as the explosion element enhanced this effect.

Some criticism was made over the fact that the Regula One space lab was the model of the orbiting office complex from ST—TMP turned upside down with some slight remodeling. The fact of the matter was that the budget on THE WRATH OF KHAN was so tight that intelligent shortcuts had to be made wherever possible. The throw the money down the rabbit hole approach of ST—TMP was an experience Paramount had no intention of ever repeating.

During the principal photography of THE WRATH OF KHAN, a camera crew from ILM, under the supervision of Jim Veilleux, visited the sound stages (stages 5, 8, 9 & 18) where the STAR TREK film was being shot. They shot background plates to facilitate the special effects process when it came time to combine opticals with live action later on. This was done using a VistaVision camera, an unusual contrivance which shoots the film in a widescreen format to make frames twice the normal size. This is important when it comes to combining elements and maintaining clarity of image between the live action and optical effects.

The VistaVision uses film at a rate twice that of a normal 35mm camera. The VistaVision camera also weighs four hundred pounds, but its weight is actually an advantage in this case. While it takes four men to move the camera whenever the position is changed, the weight insures that it creates a steady image which is vitally important in special effects photography. In special effects work, even a one-one thousandth of an inch variance can make the difference in compositing images.

Jim Veilleux's job was to supervise the animation and special computer graphics for the film. The most elaborate use of computer graphics was in the sequence showing the computer simulation of the Genesis Device. A planet is transformed by the explosion of the device on its surface. The sequence lasts about sixty seconds but represents five months of computer work by ten artists. Paramount was originally planning to use live-action footage for that sequence but what they came up with, an inorganic block being transformed into a flower, was unsatisfactory.

NEW TECHNOLOGIES

ILM developed a computer painting program which was used by matte artist Chris Evans in collaboration with computer programmer Tom Porter. They managed to program the computer so that they could paint with a light pen and get the kind of effect a painter can achieve with a brush where a stroke fades out as he applies the brush very lightly to a canvas. The computer imaging team was headed by Alvy Ray Smith and Loren Carpenter.

The effective scenes in which someone falls victim to phaser fire was photographed in an interesting manner. First the actor who was to be vaporized was photographed against a blue screen. Then the other actors who are in the same scene are photographed reacting to the actor who's being hit by phaser fire, even though that other actor is not there at the time. Then the blue screen image of the actor is superimposed over the scene with the other actors and made to dissolve. In conjunction with this there is rotoscoped artwork of the phaser effect added to complete the sequence.

Even though ILM was the special effects company ostensibly in charge of everything, they had an on-going working relationship with Peter Kuran, a former ILM technician who struck out on his own while remaining on good terms with his former employer. ILM would occasionally subcontract work to him when they were in a time crunch. Certain key phaser effects were either done or enhanced by Peter Kuran's company, Visual Concepts Engineering. The multi-beam effect when Kirk fires his phaser and destroys a Ceti Eel was the work of VCE. Kuran's crew were also called on to do the Transporter effects.

Initially Paramount wanted to use a different approach in which the figures moved as they were transporting. VCE did a number of what they call "articulate mattes" in order to accommodate this effect, but they the studio decided they wanted something different again. What evolved was the effect featuring twin pillars of light which merge as the subject is transported. Peter Kuran initially wanted to go for an effect in which a person materializes gradually so that we'd see the skeleton and circulatory system first and then the other parts of the body appearing as layers.

An example of this approach can be seen in the old OUTER LIMITS episode "The Special One". Robert Sallin talked him out of it and steered him towards the version finally pictured in the motion picture. Peter Kuran's company also added the post-production effects showing Spock being bombarded by radiation when he receives a lethal dose in engineering.

CLEAR COMMUNICATION

Producer Robert Sallin worked as the liaison between Paramount in Hollywood and ILM in Northern California. Each week ILM would provide Paramount with printouts detailing the percentage of special effects work completed to date so everyone would know exactly how the film was progressing. ILM also let Paramount know how much work remained to be finished, how much had been rejected, and so on. While ST—TMP had some five hundred special effects shots, THE WRATH OF KHAN had one hundred fifty optical effects. This film proved that less can be more as the effects presented are more exciting and tightly wound into the story. There isn't a lot of standing around looking at the view screen while nothing much happens in the plot.

Art director Mike Minor approached the new film by striving to address the failings of STAR TREK—THE MOTION PICTURE. "I thought the first movie was pretty washed out, visually," he candidly admitted in a 1982 STARLOG interview. "It had no heart. Part of that can be traced back to the design element. During the first picture, all the sets were buttoned up. In other words, the bridge was built as one, solid structure. It could never be opened up to get a camera into it for a better angle. That camera was going to be inside a real ship and we were going to wander around the vessel with it in a very slow, stately manner. That situation forced the filmmakers into a corner. They had to use very dim lighting on the sets. They couldn't let the proper amount of lights onto them because everything was so cramped."

In continuing his comparison of working on the first STAR TREK feature with the second, Minor observed, "It was a happier situation and with a closer, tighter, family. For instance, I took the Klingon bridge from the first feature and we made a study of it with my set designer, pulled it apart and we turned that into the torpedo bay where some climactic action takes place. It cost us a good bit to modify it, but it was way cheaper than building from scratch and it worked out very well. We worked out a way to utilize footage from the first feature of the Enterprise, cutting that interminable 'look-at-us-aren't-we-great-special-effects-people' trip around the Enterprise space dock, and we just used very few cuts to get us from point A to B, get inside the ship and get off on our mission."

Like many people involved in special effects, Minor had a long-standing soft spot in his heart for STAR TREK. In fact, he worked on the old TV series during its third season. "Our technical consultant, Dr. Richard Green, is also a real fan. So is Gayne Rescher, the director of photography. He really committed himself to the picture, and even came in two weeks early to work with Nick Meyer, figuring out how to shoot the bridge. People are going to notice how much more interesting the photography is in this picture because the camera is always in motion."

GETTING BACK TO BASICS

For STAR TREK II, things were restored to their former nature, as Minor explained. "They made the bridge set totally wild. All eleven sections of the bridge were unbuttoned and disconnected. We could pull sections out like you pull out slices of pie and get that camera in there on a twelve-foot crane. We could get that camera to swoop and dive and dolly and truck. There's a lot more action aboard the ship this time out. You race down the corridors. You have the image of the Enterprise whizzing right past you."

The bridge had been originally assembled as a solid piece because the director of photography on the first film thought that this would make it appear more realistic and that the actors would react in that setting more realistically. Instead the actors actually found working in such close quarters to be tight and cramped, and welcomed it when the set was opened up so that only the sections needed for a shot would be linked up for the scene they were filming. When Joe Jennings designed the bridge for ST—TMP, it was designed to come apart in wedge-shaped sections which were on wheels with hydraulic shock-absorbers. Not only did the filmmakers on ST—TMP bolt the sections together, they added a ceiling piece. All of this was undone to facilitate filming with them on THE WRATH OF KHAN.

Mike Minor worked on STAR TREK II as Art Director under Joe Jennings, who was the Production Designer. Minor had worked in a similar position on STAR TREK: THE MOTION PICTURE. In comparing the two films, Minor stated of THE WRATH OF KHAN, "For one thing the story was better. It was solved more quickly. I came on board and my first function was to sit down and lay out the storyboard. I was laying out the boards while they were tying the story down." In order to prepare a précis of the special effects so that companies could bid on doing them, Mike Minor had to storyboard them all. He was working on them while the script was being rewritten and wound up doing storyboards for four different versions of STAR TREK II. He remarked once that he must have put four hundred man hours into those storyboards before they reached the final version.

A preliminary estimate and time study was done on how long it should take to do the effects. They had to start the effects as quickly as possible with Industrial Light & Magic and so they made two or three trips up there to discuss the look of things. Minor sat down with Sallin and put a few ideas in. For instance, it was Mike Minor's idea to place the climax of the picture in the Mutara Nebula. Minor had been trying to get them to use nebulas previously back in STAR TREK—THE MOTION PICTURE.

HI-TECH MEETS THE COW PALACE

The way it turned out, the nebula was used to very good effect for screen tension as well as for its dynamic visual appeal. By using a colorful nebula, they got out of the usual black space and white stars and got into colored realms. The two big space galleons could lumber toward and away from each other and drift into opacities and come out through translucent veils of color and it was very attractive and worked out well.

The climactic space battle inside the nebula was filmed inside a huge building just outside San Francisco called the Cow Palace. The explosion which creates the Genesis planet was also filmed there and was created by Thaine Morris. A great deal of footage must be shot for such effects and in one week they shot thirty-five thousand feet. A high speed camera enabled them to slow down the action by actually filming at the rate of 2,400 frames per second as opposed to the normal 24 frames per second. Other technicians who worked on this sequence include cameraman Don Dow, and camera assistants Selwyn Eddy and Mike Owens.

The nebula effect was achieved using a cloud tank, a very old process which works remarkably well. Many filmgoers are most familiar with the type of unusual cloud effects seen in such films as CLOSE ENCOUNTERS OF THE THIRD KIND, POLTERGEIST and RAIDERS OF THE LOST ARK. However, a nebula effect such as the one seen in STAR TREK II had never been attempted. The cloud tank at ILM was four feet by eight feet and resembled a huge aquarium. They first put fresh water in the tank and then carefully add salt water on top of it.

An inversion layer is created where the two layers of water meet and begin to mix. The actual clouds are achieved by adding a solution of white rubber latex which is carefully injected into the slowly swirling water using meat basters with long tubes. The colors of the clouds are changed by shining different colored lights on them as they're filmed, thus achieving such diverse shades as magenta, orange, green, yellow and cobalt blue.

A small pump in the cloud tank causes the water to move slowly and thus create the slowly swirling shapes which the clouds acquire. These shapes can maintain themselves for hours or pass within minutes. The film crew has to be ready to get the camera going and the lights on at a moments notice should the tank produce something especially unusual and strange. The cloud tank was shot at the rate of one frame per second, so the long exposure enabled the image to be manipulated in other ways.

ANYTHING GOES

Special effects co-supervisor Ken Ralston could walk around the tank and shine a light into it at specific points and thereby create lighting effects which on film come across as discharges of energy in the nebula. In order to match these lighting effects to the models, he'd do what he called "lightning passes" across the models of the Enterprise or the Reliant with spotlights. The cloud tank was just one element which would later have to be combined with other elements involving the starfield, phaser fire and the ships themselves.

The explosion of the Reliant was complicated in and of itself. Flaming pieces of debris were photographed blue screen as four separate elements. For each of those elements, they filmed a separate flashing light and burning spark element to match up to it when the pieces were composited into one scene. Other elements which had to be composited into the one shot included the ship, the nebula and the stars visible in the nebula. Including the explosions as well, eighteen different pieces of film were combined in an optical printer for a scene which on screen is only about two seconds long.

The Enterprise went through some changes at ILM where they shot all their effects work against blue screen rather than against black, which is the way Trumbull had done it. That process gave them some problems because if you get any shine on the surface of the model when you're shooting blue screen, you've got a hole in the film positive. For this reason, they had to repaint the surface of the model to dull it down, although it looks no different on screen than it did in ST—TMP. Because of the problems they had working with the heavy model, ILM put in a request to EEG to borrow some crew people (at ILM's expense). Trumbull refused any sort of cooperation.

In spite of the problems they had working with the Enterprise model, production designer Joe Jennings believed that it was a design which was an essential part of STAR TREK. While some found the Reliant a more pleasing shape, Jennings said of the Enterprise in an interview in the July 1982 CINEFANTASTIQUE, "We were stuck with that schematic, but I think we *should* be stuck with it. It's part of the STAR TREK universe now. The fans are familiar with how the Enterprise looks, so it all has a sort of *de facto* existence, a bogus logic. You have to work with that, and I think a production designer has to realize it. Directors, too. Sometimes they're hard to convince and you have to do a sales job. You have to say, 'Look, that won't work, that place isn't there. You can't get there from here and the fans know it. If you want to do your own outer space movie then go off and do it, but don't call it STAR TREK."

THE "CAN-OPENER"

A particularly impressive special effects shot involving the Enterprise was conceived by Mike Minor and he called it the "can-opener" shot. That happens as the Enterprise meets the Reliant head-on in the nebula and he says, 'Evasive action starboard,' the Enterprise pulls starboard and it's caught by a beam which slashes across the base of the dorsal. You see the beam tracing along the miniature detail of the Enterprise, tearing it open, only they don't linger long enough to see what it caused. Minor called it the can-opener shot because you see the hull splitting open as the beam eats along it. This was filmed using a large section of the Enterprise built showing just the section which was to be damaged. It was constructed out of wax which, as they planned, softened under the hot lights used in filming. Sculpting tools were used to open holes in the hull which were ostensibly being made by phaser fire.

Then they cut to the interior and you see the torpedo bay full size filled with people in flame and the walls bursting apart. They originally thought that the filmmakers were going to tear the wall open and have guys yanked out on wires. But again, budget, time and effects prevented this complicated shot. Minor also came up with the shot where the Reliant just comes right out of the water, so to speak, and right over our heads as it clears the top of the Enterprise. "That got a good yelp out of the sound technicians when they were previewing the film to lay the sound effects," Minor recalled. "It got some good yelps in the theatre, too. I was happy with that shot.

"All in all," Minor continued, "ILM thought the picture had a good kinetic feeling about it. I felt vindicated in my choices of how to shoot the ships when they'd done it so well and made us look good. People seem to like the Reliant. Our producers, Bennett and Sallin, felt that the

Reliant was a better looking ship than the Enterprise. I don't necessarily agree or disagree. It's just different. I think it's clean and workmanlike. That's something that Joe (Jennings) and I came up with simultaneously. I detailed the ship and worked on the working drawings with Lee Cole. We drafted that and got full sets of full-sized blueprints.

"We had to make budgetary considerations," Minor admitted. "We were disappointed in that we wanted to make Kirk's quarters two-levels, looking out on San Francisco. We wanted to see him coming up the stairs from the bottom level. We had to build it on one level and cut $40 thousand out of that set. With one thing and another, I felt happy that I could at least get two miniature buildings thrown out against the backdrop. They're just a throw-away, but the elevator is going up and down past him in that opening sequence in the apartment at night. There's something going on in the middleground so you believe what's outside the window a bit more, hopefully." When Kirk is in his quarters and outside we can see the San Francisco of the future at night, this was accomplished by putting miniature buildings in front of a painted cyclorama of the distant landscape. It makes for a very convincing and effective sequence, particularly with the added touch of lighted elevators moving up the side of the miniature.

RECYCLING

The eighty foot cyclorama was not painted new for the film but was another retread. It was obtained from 20th Century Fox and had been used in THE TOWERING INFERNO, also to represent San Francisco. The backlit scene of the city lights across San Francisco Bay fit in flawlessly. The set of Kirk's apartment was constructed on stage 8 which made use of an existing lower level beneath the stage floor which formed the area outside the apartment windows.

"It's always tough getting the effects and the miniature tied together for a live-action shot. Those were made up totally of pieces left over from the first picture. In fact, we cannibalized more sets from the first picture. There was more stuff thrown away in that first picture; whole sets that cost hundreds of thousands that never made it to the screen." These included sets for the spacewalk scene with Kirk and Spock involving a Memory Wall. "Those were just jettisoned. They were dreadful. But there were parts from those sets, thousands of bucks worth of pre-cast plastic and things and we used them all to dress up the Enterprise and the other ship. There was enough to build a whole condominium with sets that were thrown out of the first picture."

Lee Cole, the graphics expert who worked with Mike Minor on the film, agreed. "Because of the budget, we recycled every fragment of the old sets for this movie. That was quite a challenge. In this movie, the Enterprise has a different look. We cut the Klingon set from the first film in half. Part of it is now the torpedo room aboard the Enterprise. Part of it became the Transporter room of the space station. I very carefully had to cut out all the Klingon writing."

For all the budgetary restrictions on this particular film project, Cole pointed out that Paramount probably got more for their money than on the previous STAR TREK feature. "You see more of the ship in this film. You see the torpedo room. You see the inner workings of sick bay. You see the living quarters. We also improved the bridge quite a bit. We added a lot of detailing. Nick Meyer loved little flashing lights and do-dads."

The video monitors on the bridge were altered and brought up to speed so that they didn't present the problems that the director of ST—TMP had to deal with. As Lee Cole explained, "We removed all the rear-projection film set-ups from the first movie. They never really showed up that well. We installed real video units. That was a real job because there we no existing video TV's that would fit in that console. We had to custom build a video system. We now have real video units all over the bridge and throughout the medical lab. About one third of the material you'll see on the screens was made by me at the Jet Propulsion Laboratories."

VIDEO VS. FILM

Cole worked in conjunction with video engineers Ed Moscowitz and Jim Padget to produce video images which were done in phase with the movement of motion picture film. The images didn't flicker but maintained their clarity when reproduced in the motion picture. These video images were also easier to rewind and replay than the 16mm film loops used on the screen in ST—TMP.

Effects supervisor Ken Ralston was less than sanguine about the hardware used in the film. "I hate the Enterprise model," he swore. "I think it's made out of lead. It took eight guys to mount it for a shot and a forklift to move it around.

"The ship won't look any different on the screen," Ralston continued, referring to the extra detailing and rougher texture he added to the leftover (and weighty) model. "The iridescence effect still works, but having a little relief on the surface made things easier on us. We didn't have to horse around with the lighting to get rid of gloss.

"I'll probably get attacked about this, but I'm just not crazy about the original design of the Enterprise. It's a shape that does not lend itself easily to looking good in the frame. It's hard to come up with angles that really read like anything. There are only two good angles on it. The Reliant is a nice, squat contraption that looks a lot more believable to me. The ship takes the best of the Enterprise, rearranges it, and adds a few goodies of its own. And the model is great. It's made of vacu-formed plastic and two guys can mount it on the pipes for a shot."

"We redesigned the Enterprise for the Reliant," Lee Cole explained. "It's the Enterprise with a roll bar. It has a photon cannon and a lot of military looking details. The Reliant is designed to look like an earlier model starship because the Enterprise is supposed to be the state of the art in terms of starship technology.

A different kind of special effects work was used to convey the sense that an indoor set on a sound stage was actually a location shot. Due to the stormy nature of the surface of the planet, blowing sand and an obscured background enabled the desolate landscape under a hot sun to be duplicated indoors when the surface of Ceti Alpha Five was created. This was built inside stage 8 on the Paramount lot.

A number of frames were built on the sound stage to construct the set and to create hills and sand mounds. These were covered with sand and fuller's earth. The fuller's earth was blown around by four huge Ritter fans (which resemble caged airplane propellers) to create the look of a sand storm. There were sixty foot sand dunes which dropped off abruptly at a forty-five degree angle to continue offstage where they were obscured by the blowing fuller's earth. The backdrop of the sound stage was a huge painted cyclorama of a storm swept sky.

A BAD DECISION

Originally the script called for an ice planet but Joe Jennings and Mike Minor decided that from a design standpoint a desert planet would be more interesting. After three days of blowing dirt they regretted that decision. The actors weren't that crazy about it either. Their spacesuits weren't ventilated and once the helmets were fastened on the suits only had five minutes of air in them. Between takes, a hose had to be shoved under the helmets to refill the suits with fresh air.

The long shots of planets seen in the film are miniatures. There were two versions made of the exterior of Gamma Regula, the planet were Khan tries to maroon Kirk. A half-sphere was built for long shots with landscape details painted on. For close-up shots where the details had to look more realistic, a three hundred pound section of the planet was constructed on a table-top which allowed the camera to pass over it, thereby creating the illusion that it passing over a real planet's surface.

A unique element in the film was the Ceti Eel, the small creatures which could burrow into a person's head, ostensibly wrap themselves around a person's cerebral cortex, and leave them open to hypnotic suggestion. Early versions of the script had a creature which was attached to the back of a person's neck, but producer Robert Sallin thought that idea was old hat He wanted something which would get a more visceral reaction from the audience. When Sallin saw a slug on his sidewalk one morning, it gave him the idea for the Ceti Eel. And even though the creature doesn't really look like an eel, the name stuck. Sallin discussed his idea with Ken Ralston at ILM, who came up with some sketches of the creature.

The model of the adult eel was fourteen inches long and the offspring were made in several sizes. The adult is shown in the scene when one of the offspring is removed from beneath the shell. For this scene the eel adult was a puppet made with rods beneath the tail section which moved it and gave it the illusion of life. There was also a separate mechanism for moving the creature's jaws. The baby eels were made from foam rubber and pulled along via a mono-filament line which was invisible on camera. The Ceti eel tank was constructed so that the rod puppets could be operated from beneath it through special slots. The plastic base of the tank was painted the same color as the sand the eels moved through so that the plastic base wouldn't show through the sand.

ALL BABIES AREN'T CUTE

The scenes where Walter Koenig and Paul Winfield had the baby eels crawling on their faces inside the helmets were actually filmed at Ken Ralston's shop. The baby eel models had to be covered in a special goo so that they seemed to leave a slimy trail behind them like a snail. The only part of the experience Walter Koenig was bothered by was when they had to film the eel, and its accompanying goo, on his ear. The actual close-up of the eel emerging from Chekov's ear was done with an oversized model of his ear. The adult eel, covered with slime, was used here as though it was one of the baby eels since the close-up called for larger scale. They did three versions of this scene. One with no blood, one with a little blood and one with a great deal of blood (what they called the *Fangoria* shot).

A key element of the plot for STAR TREK II was thought up by Mike Minor, although he did not receive any writing credit. Originally the script didn't have anything like the Genesis Device. It had the Omega System, a powerful explosive which Khan was after. "Harve wanted something uplifting," Minor told CINEFANTASTIQUE magazine in the July-August 1982 issue, "something that would be as fundamental in the twenty-third century as the discovery of recombinant DNA is in our time."

Minor continued, "Then something just came to me, and I said, 'Terraforming.' Harve asked, 'What's that?' and I told him it was the altering of existing planets to conditions which are compatible to human life. I suggested a plot, just making it up in my head while talking on the phone. . . the Federation had developed a way of engineering the planetary evolution of a body in space on such a rapid scale that instead of eons you have events taking place in months or years. You pick a dead world or an inhospitable gas planet, and you change its genetic matrix or code, thereby speeding up time. This, of course, is a terrible weapon—suppose you trained it on a planet filled with people and speeded up its evolution? You could destroy the planet and every life form on it. The Federation is involved with playing God, but at the same time, trying to take barren dead worlds and convert them into lovely worlds. Harve liked the idea a lot. At the story conference the next day, he came over, hugged me, and said, 'You saved STAR TREK!' "

This led to the various elements of the Genesis planet, most notably the Genesis Cave. The portion of the cave we see the actors in is just a small set on a Paramount sound stage—the rest is special effects. It was made to resemble a piece of a huge bubble since it was felt that the energy released by the Genesis Device would be capable of melting rock. Mike Minor and Joe Jennings agreed that the bubble look should somewhat resemble that used in the caves in the 1953 science fiction film INVADERS FROM MARS.

RULE #1: USE ALL RESOURCES

The half-bubble was made by a company which ordinarily specializes in making domed swimming pool covers. It's made from Fiberglas which was carved and painted to look like part of the cave. The vegetation close to the half-bubble was part of the set but then this blended in various matte paintings which formed the larger image.

The various matte paintings in the Genesis Cave sequence were done by Chris Evans and Frank Ordaz. They created the illusion of a huge waterfall, mist and sunlight sparkling on an underground lake, so elements in the background actually moved. The illusion of sunlight streaming through the clouds was achieved through the use of a half-silvered mirror which was placed between the matte painting and the camera at a forty-five degree angle to the camera lens. The mirror reflected light into the lens while the mirror remained invisible on film other than as reflected light. The light shaft effect was achieved by drawing chalk lines on black paper and photographed so that only the lines are superimposed over the other images.

The moving waterfall was achieved through the use of a rotating wheel. The painting of the waterfall was done and then the water motion effect was managed by having cotton on the wheel moving behind cut-out shapes of the water channels. The painting of the area around it was done without the waterfall, which was double-exposed and added later. So several different elements combined to complete that scene. Those working on it wanted to spend more time refining the images, but time was the one thing they didn't have. The result, while passable, is not as impressive as the technicians would have preferred. The cave was also supposed to continue the bubble motif of the melted rock but this wasn't done either, much to Mike Minor's disappointment.

Production began on THE WRATH OF KHAN November 9, 1981 and wrapped on January 2, 1982. After post production work was completed, the film was released on June 4, 1982. Meyer encountered some interesting problems during this period between the start of production and the actual release of the film.

First there were the technical demands of working on the set, which is a difficult set to shoot. Most of the action takes place on that bridge, which is a three-hundred-and-sixty degree set. This means a lot of coverage has to be filmed (coverage being the same scenes from different angles), and that can get rather boring. The set was Fiberglas so they had to tape things which were always coming down. Plus it's hard to light there. There were technical problems, but every film presents some technical problems.

NOT ENOUGH TIME

"Making the film was very, very hard," Meyer stated. "One of the hardest things I ever did. I think one of the things that made it so much harder than it needed to be was that before we rolled the camera, Paramount had booked this movie into umpteen hundred theaters on June 4 [1982], which I didn't know. That didn't give much post-production time, the time used to complete the film. I can only contrast it with TIME AFTER TIME. We finished shooting the movie Thanksgiving 1978 and the movie was released in October 1979, so I had, in effect, a year to finish the film." But the director actually spent five months editing that earlier film. "Editing is where films really get made. Dailies are like sentences in a book which hasn't been written yet. Editing is that process of trial and error, and also of contemplation. A five-month editing period is very useful for a movie. You can try things and change things and experiment and play around. I had a year to do it.

"We finished shooting [THE WRATH OF KHAN] February first and the film had to be shot during the day and edited at night. Normally, if this was George Lucas, we'd have a year to do that. But we had a month. I had two and a half weeks to edit the movie. When I discovered this was going to be the case, what happened was, in order to give myself a few more weeks, the film had to be shot during the day and edited at night and on weekends. That meant that for the period of six weeks plus, I had the curious experience of never seeing the light of day.

"I would go to work at about five-thirty or six o'clock, before the sun had come up. I would eat lunch in a dark theatre looking at my dailies, so I'd never see the sunshine then. At night we would come out of the sound stages and I would go off to the editing room, by which time it was dark. On weekends I would also get up before sunrise and go down to the editing room. I wondered whether I would physically be able to stand it because I was putting in eighteen-hour days, seven days a week. That part of it was not fun. The shooting of it continued to be fun, but that was played against exhaustion.

"I will never make a movie again in which I don't know beforehand that there is enough time to finish the film. We were such a photo-finish that we started printing the film—to make sixteen hundred prints takes three weeks in itself so count backwards from June fourth to May tenth or something like that—and then there were special effects coming in. ILM would send us down pieces of film with a label on it, shot 36A, and we would have to match that angle with shooting it. My cut of the movie when it was first put together was a fifty-percent 'scene missing' or 'insert missing.' Kirk would say 'Fire,' and then 'scene missing.' It made it very hard to tell about the movie.

TECHNICAL DIFFICULTIES

"Basically, changing the film is no big deal," Meyer continued. "Theoretically, you could keep changing right up until you print. But you will affect the sound. Sound effects are made up of many tracks. So if a reel of film is a thousand feet long and somewhere four hundred and thirty-odd feet in, somebody knocks on the door, there's a separate reel of film that is black for four hundred and thirty-seven feet, there's a knock, and black for the rest of the reel. That is completely separate. Ray guns or whatever we're talking about are all on separate tracks. So you have as many as fifty or more separate soundtracks for the same reel of film.

"What sound people keep hounding you for are 'locked reels' (finished reels). My problem was that I was deprived of that period called contemplation, when you play with the film. If you suddenly have an Epiphany, 'Gee, I know now I can make it ten times better. Just remove thirteen frames from Spock opening his eyes so he opens them a little faster,' or something at the beginning of the movie— that's hell to do that, and it costs a fortune."

After Meyer had completed the film, a crew from ILM, under the direction of Robert Sallin, shot news scenes in April 1982 at Golden Gate Park in San Francisco. These scenes show Spock's torpedo casing coffin at rest in the jungle, thereby creating a more hopeful ending. Meyer's version had the casket ejected into space and that was the last we'd see of it. These scenes were supposedly shot as a result of test screenings in which Spock's death seemed too absolute and depressing.

"Paramount was a little apprehensive about killing a major character," Shatner explained in the November 1982 issue of FANTASTIC FILMS. "They wanted to have something else they could use in case the death of Spock didn't work. No other ending was contemplated, but that last shot was kind of manipulated a little bit. Instead of being shot into space, which was the original concept, it was decided to make the sarcophagus land in the lush fields of the Genesis effect. That was the only adjustment, but it was a key adjustment."

That adjustment was so key that it was strenuously objected to by director Nicholas Meyer, who revealed in the December 1991 CINEFANTASTIQUE just how hard he fought against the change. "I fought very hard to make him dead, and the shots that imply a resurrection—the vision of the casket on the genesis planet—were done over my dead body, with my strenuous objection. I objected so strenuously, and went to such lengths, that a producer on the film referred to me as morally bankrupt. He said, 'You'd walk over your mother to get this the way you wanted,' and I said, 'You know I think you're right.' "

The reason Nicholas Meyer didn't get his way regarding the final scene was that it was the idea of Harve Bennett, and he held firm once his mind was made up. The new scenes were directed by Robert Sallin who also chose the location for them. The sequence is only sixty seconds long but leaves open many possibilities, as STAR TREK III: THE SEARCH FOR SPOCK well proved.

The Search for Spock

Ⅰn the aftermath of STAR TREK II: THE WRATH OF KHAN, Paramount Studio hired Leonard Nimoy to direct the sequel to what had at one point seemed to be his farewell to the TREK universe. To catch and hold the interest of diehard audiences perturbed by the perceived assassination of their Vulcan hero, Paramount even called the new movie THE SEARCH FOR SPOCK. Of course, it really didn't take too much imagination to sense that the Genesis planet might just *possibly* hold the key to preventing Spock from staying dead. The question was, how would the inevitable crowd-pleasing resurrection be presented?

The answer, of course, was: *SPECIAL EFFECTS!* And what a plethora of special effects it would be: more spaceships, another look at the space dock, an examination of Klingon household pets, strange weather on the Genesis planet, huge microbes, big worms, even bigger, slimier worms, the destruction of an entire planet tearing itself apart, and, in yet another controversial plot move guaranteed to truly vex dyed-in-the-wool TREK fanatics, the utter destruction of the U.S.S. Enterprise NCC-1701! A full four million of STAR TREK III's sixteen million dollar budget— a staggering twenty-five per cent— was allocated directly for the special effects budget.

It came as no surprise that STAR TREK III: THE SEARCH FOR SPOCK would mark the continuation of Industrial Light and Magic's fruitful involvement with STAR TREK. This time, however, ILM was to be more closely involved in the filmmaking process from the very beginning. On the previous STAR TREK II: THE WRATH OF KHAN, the renowned effects company had simply been presented with a set of already completed storyboards, and they were thus obliged to work the visual special effects out from those.

This time around, in the case of STAR TREK III, effects supervisor Ken Ralston worked out the effects storyboards in collaboration with Nilo Rodis and David Carson. All the Genesis sets, a new Earth space drydock, the U.S.S. Grissom, the U.S.S. Excelsior and the Klingon ship were all derived from ILM's original design sketches as well. Industrial Light and Magic would, at the final tally, create over one hundred and twenty complete special visual effects shots for STAR TREK III: THE SEARCH FOR SPOCK.

Beyond this central core of effects wizards, most everyone was pretty much in the dark regarding the plot of THE SEARCH FOR SPOCK. The effects teams were only given sections of the script, and out of sequence at that.

TIGHT SECURITY

The same situation applied on the Paramount set. Designers and builders were all kept *out* of the know. Security at both Paramount and Industrial Light and Magic was incredibly close in order to avoid leaks, theft and rumors. Of course, STAR TREK III was not ILM's sole security concern at the time. When STAR TREK III art director John Chilberg visited ILM, he was ushered ceremoniously into the locked room where the STAR TREK III storyboards were pinned to the wall. He was also told not to look at the storyboards on the *other* wall.

Those storyboards were for yet another secret effects project, Steven Spielberg's INDIANA JONES AND THE TEMPLE OF DOOM. And by and large, the security at Industrial Light and Magic was a considerable deal more efficient than that at the Paramount lot, where costumes from the film were difficult to keep track of, and frequently turned up missing. (To make matters worse, William Shatner's expanding waistline required new costumes for him on a regular basis. This was one special effect that was way beyond the powers of Industrial Light and Magic!)

By and large, the costumes for STAR TREK III were costumes that had already seen service in STAR TREK II and only needed a little work to emerge from mothballs— provided that they hadn't already been stolen. Costume refurbishment, as well as new costume design, was done by Paramount's Robert Fletcher, a veteran costume designer with considerable STAR TREK experience . And a wealth of eclectic knowledge of clothing design that served him well.

For instance, in the case of the costume worn by Ambassador Sarek when he visits Admiral Kirk, Fletcher based his design on the stone-studded breastplate worn by the High Priest of the ancient Jews. For the Klingon costumes worn by Christopher Lloyd, John Larroquette and the other Klingons of STAR TREK III, Fletcher also referred back to the clothing of another ancient historical era: feudal Japan. Any plans to re-use any leftover Klingon costumes from STAR TREK: THE MOTION PICTURE were effectively squashed by the discovery that only six survived, and that these had been damaged beyond any effective repair— in an episode of MORK AND MINDY!

(Trivia buffs should note that these costumes can be observed in a pile of space junk in a MORK AND MINDY episode from the final season which features Jonathan Winters as Mork's son.)

ALWAY INTERESTING

For the scene where McCoy becomes unhinged in a futuristic bar, the effects team devised a computer generated video game which featured the amusing anachronism of World War One bi-planes recreated as part of a holographic tabletop entertainment. Although almost all the props in THE SEARCH FOR SPOCK were especially constructed for the film, the barroom scene did have one Twentieth-Century artifact on hand: a drinking glass with a swirl straw. The set for this entire sequence was actually the Enterprise sick bay, redressed to look like a not-too-seedy watering hole of the Twenty-third century, from a design by set designer Cameron Birnie.

At the live action end of things, a few changes were made on the Enterprise set. Production designer John Chilberg discovered that the floor of the Enterprise bridge set was painted black and did not photograph well; it did not reflect any light whatsoever. So, Chilberg had his crew tone the floor down by repainting it a dark gray .

Principal photography for STAR TREK III was completed on October 21, 1983. As noted, the all-important task of fleshing out the existing gaps in the film's images went to George Lucas' ILM. Said director Leonard Nimoy of this amazing special effects studio: "I found the people at Industrial Light and Magic totally supportive and wildly imaginative. They are film lovers. They want to be turned on, just like the actors. They have a high-tech background, but they never employed their knowledge to coerce or manipulate me."

ILM's production supervisor Warren Franklin revealed, in a 1984 interview, what that entailed for him and his team. He felt, and justifiably so, that STAR TREK III was a perfect project for Industrial Light and Magic. He, along with the two art directors (David Carson and Nilo Rodis) were very pleased to be involved in the film making process from the very beginning of the project.

Beginning in November of 1982, when they first received the original two-page outline that Harve Bennett had written, Franklin, Rodis and Carson began storyboarding the movie and the effects shots. They added what they could even though some of the special effects sequences had already been fairly well worked up by Paramount's team in advance.

A TEAM EFFORT

Rodis, Carson and Franklin worked very closely with Nimoy and producer Harve Bennett, and also with Paramount's artist, Tom Lay. These men worked together all the way through the script, scene-by-scene, in effect storyboarding not only the effects sequences but also the non-effects sequences so that the look of the STAR TREK III: THE SEARCH FOR SPOCK would be very integrated. They also did the key illustrations for all the main sets on the Genesis planet, and they also designed the new Excelsior spaceship, the Bird of Prey, the new scout-class vehicle the Grissom, and the new space dock in Earth orbit.

Working from these sketches, modelmakers such as Bill George and Michael Fulmer came up with rough prototype designs. These were later developed in the model-making workshops until they reached their final design form. This process of designing-in-the-shop gave the effects team an effective head start in knowing just what they were going to need to work with. This created a considerable advantage in terms of preparation time.

In the course of this design process, Fulmer and some of the other ILM model makers would generally come up with quick little prototypes that helped everyone get a much clearer idea of what the production was in need of. Fulmer recalled that many of the models were put through an extensive brainstorming process. In one specific case, a certain space station design seemed to be getting pretty close to what the production office wanted but a few changes were necessary. This space station design was then handed over to Bill George, who whipped up the specified alterations in about half an hour. Then the design team would converse about it again and change it some more.

This collective process produced a sort of 'visual sketching' that gave the Industrial Light and Magic effects and model team a direction to head for, and a much greater clarity in the development of the models in question. This process was implemented because both Paramount and ILM wanted to get as much of STAR TREK III's design locked down at the beginning of the production as they could. This kept things rolling ahead as smoothly as possible.

In order to avoid blank spaces in the footage being worked with by Nimoy and his editing team, special effects editors Jay Ignaszewski and Bill Kimberlin provided "rough" effects footage: black and white footage of the effects shots, indicating their appearance when completed, but without supporting structures removed from the shots. This allowed editing to go on even while the effects shots were being polished for their ultimate on-screen appearances.

AN "ARDUOUS PROCESS"

Effects photographer Scott Farrar recalled working on the sequence in which the battle-scarred Enterprise returns to space dock. He and his team had spent their first few months simply creating footage of the interior portions of the space dock. They did not have any complex moves to film. However, getting even the relatively static interior spacedock shots together was very time consuming. Getting all the various required passes of the miniature "set" was an extremely arduous process.

To further complicate matters, it was necessary to use smoke inside the spacedock model to create the crucial illusion of depth. Farrar and his associates tested a lot of different looks to make the interior of the dock seem appropriately vast. They discovered that the interior of the space dock required some degree of atmospheric haze (even though, scientifically speaking, there probably wouldn't be any in outer space). The basic concept was to use smoke to help the image look slightly degraded, rather than pristine and clear.

As a result, they ended up using blue gels on the lights and shooting in smoke for the basic 'fill' look. Then, when Farrar went to the filming of the light passes, he and his team employed a diffusion filter on his camera. They could have employed smoke here as well, but because the light passes were so long, they would have to have had a system where the smoke level could somehow have been constantly controlled. This would have been much more difficult and time consuming under the circumstances of the production schedule, so Farrar opted not to use smoke in that sequence after all.

Farrar also discovered that it simply was not possible to shoot any of the ship models actually *in* the space dock because none of the models' scales matched. If the scales had been the same, a great deal of time and money could have been saved by filming the spaceships and the space dock together, but it was not to be so.

The first spaceship sequence filmed at ILM was that of the Enterprise floating out of the space dock. This was a relatively straightforward shot and posed no problems. The effects photographers could get away with a lot in this sequence, since the Enterprise was moving in the shot. But they found themselves faced with an extremely difficult undertaking. The ships were supposed to remain stationary, relative to the dock wall, while the camera itself was moving. They shot a lot of black-and-white tests—practice shots, basically—in their efforts to lock the ships in with the spacedock background. They had to plot each shot out on the Movieola editing machine, point to point on a grid system. It had to look like the ships were glued to the spacedock wall as any visible movement would have utterly destroyed the illusion that the ships were immobile in space.

A HECTIC PACE

The dock sequence took a couple of months to complete. As fast as Farrar and his team could complete the background, Don Dow would immediately start plugging in ships for the shot. Every once in a while, he and his team would break out of that procedure in order to photograph another ship at the opposite end of the motion control track. Even with these time saving procedures and doubling up on hours, the pace was hectic for everyone in every aspect of the special effects production.

The basic lighting of the space dock model interior was an extremely complicated set up. First, there were lights outside the space dock to light all the pinholes in the body of the model. In addition to that light source, there were extensive fiber optics liberally applied to the model. On top of all these light sources, the model builders had also applied a considerable number of miniature practical lights on the inside of the dock model. The combination of all those things gave the space dock its 'lit' look from wall to ceiling to floor.

The effects team discovered that when the dock's doors opened, they would obscure the pinhole lights, so they would have to run fiber optics beneath the doors to the wall that would be covered up otherwise. After all, the pinholes were *meant* to represent interior lights, not actual holes in the space dock. The trick that faced the effects team here was to always match the lighting and make sure there weren't any flares going into the lens from all the different angles of the lights they had sitting there.

In some cases, they had eighteen stage lights running outside, and they had to have the fans blowing constantly on the outside of the space dock to keep everything cool. Otherwise, the heat from the high-intensity light sources could distort all of the detailed artwork on the inside of the space dock wall, effectively destroying it. The space dock doors themselves were supposed to have some brightly lit panels inside them, so the doors required a separate light pass of their own. They had a rig that was actually mounted on the door—lights aimed into the boxes built onto the door, so the cinematographer could get an evenly toned light on the translucent material.

Although most of the special effects for STAR TREK III were done at ILM's facilities, some of the effects were filmed at the Paramount lot. Some of these included the Klingon commander's bizarre dog-like pet (filmed live on the set with Christopher Lloyd) and his later struggle with the killer worms of Genesis. Ralston and his Industrial Light and Magic team worked closely with the Paramount crew on these sequences. The collaboration was a notable success.

MAN'S BEST FRIEND

Commander Kruge's bizarre Klingon pet, a reptilian canine of sorts, was created by Ken Ralston. Its realization on screen was primarily the work of David Sosalla in conjunction with John Reed and Kirk Thatcher. Sosalla, a top creator of creatures for film, was perhaps best known in the effects field and beyond for his work with puppeteer Chris Walas on the motion picture GREMLINS. While the lizard-dog's body was activated by the usual assemblage of cables and air bladders, the head was operated by Ken Ralston manually.

Ralston's arm entered the lizard-dog puppet through one side of the body, away from camera view. Ralston's thumb operated a sensitive spring mechanism which produced movements of the creature's jaw. Ralston operated the creature from a cramped vantage point directly beneath the command chair occupied by Christopher Lloyd as Commander Kruge. The three remote operators in charge of the cable-and-air-assisted movements of the creature had a somewhat more comfortable task, as they were able to watch and respond to Ralston's hand movements on video monitors, adding the detailed "acting" movements— nose, eye, lip and breathing movements among them—to flesh out Ralston's work and bring the creature to cinematic life. The puppet was actually stationary, but careful movements made it seem ready to raise itself up from its comfortable spot at it's master's feet at any given moment.

Ultimately, the lizard-dog perished. For this scene, a "dead" version of the creature was designed, only to be supplanted at the last moment by its articulated "live" counterpart at the last moment, sufficiently reworked to cover up the puppeteer's arm-hole in its side.

Other details on board the Klingon ship were designed by Paramount's production artist Tom Lay. One intriguing item in particular was his original design: the medical examination table in the sick bay of Commander Kruge's Bird of Prey. The table was built to resemble the outline of a serpent with its head coiled over the head of the patient, which would seem to suggest that the Klingon physician's bedside manner is based on an entirely different set of philosophical premises than those of his human counterpart! As if that weren't enough, the instrument panel over the diagnostic bed was blood red and shaped like a serpent's mouth, and the side of the bed was fully equipped with fangs!

TRAVEL COMES WITH THE JOB

Director Nimoy, with cast and crew, actually traveled to the Industrial Light and Magic facility in Marin County to shoot one scene. The scene involved a conversation in the Starfleet dockside cafeteria, with a window looking out upon the seemingly vast space dock as a background to the expository dialogue. Ken Ralston recalled how it was accomplished: "The cafeteria scene has a live-action foreground that's a set they did here at Industrial Light and Magic with about forty extras. On top of that, a matte painting is added to complete the rest of the cafeteria from the inside. Through the window, you see the Enterprise, which is a miniature composited in later, and behind that you see the back side of the space dock. It's a tremendous shot; you get all this scope and scale that doesn't occur most of the time, and they could only do a shot like that because of the very large blue screen they have here at Industrial Light and Magic."

Ken Ralston also recalled the considerable length of some of the special effects shots the ILM team had to put together for STAR TREK III. According to Ralston, they were exceedingly long shots comprised of anywhere between four and five hundred frames. (Most of the effects shots in the STAR WARS films, which Ralston had also worked on, rarely consisted of more than one hundred frames, and most STAR WARS shots actually averaged out at about twenty frames in length.) Short shots are easier because the effects artists can get away with less detail and precision for a shot that whips right past the audience's frame of perception only to be replaced by some other dazzlingly fast visual effect.

If the matter did not fit exactly right, the audience was not going to see it anyway. If it was against a star field, and it's there and gone so quickly that viewer's mind cannot detect any big errors in the shot, then its okay to for the effects team to slack off just a bit, at least. But in the long duration shots, every single detail was lit and the ships were composited against a light background to boot. If the mattes in these sequences were not executed absolutely flawlessly, then the resulting error in matte lines would have been all-too-painfully obvious to every single person who watched the sequence.

In this manner, the use of the term "magic" to describe special visual effects of the sort created by Industrial Light and Magic and other effects companies is not at all misleading; like a professional stage magician, the effects wizards also use fast movement and misdirection, sometimes, to create the illusion of something that is not real. However, Ralston and his team did not have that luxury in many sequences of STAR TREK III. Their work was to be held up in the air for everyone in the world to scrutinize at their leisure! Ralston recalled with some chagrin one matte painting near the end of the film which had to stay on screen for a rather long time, and even though the matte was flawlessly done, Ralston was still nervous when the film was screened; to his professional eye, the time that this matte was on screen seemed like long excruciating minutes rather than one or two dozen seconds.

DESTRUCTION OF THE ENTERPRISE

The most spectacular effect in the film, and certainly the most controversial, was the destruction of the Enterprise. Even the technicians at ILM, whose job it was to do the actual blowing up of the ship, had mixed feelings the demolition of such a cultural icon. Special Effects Supervisor Ken Ralston had this to say in the November 1984 issue of FANTASTIC FILMS.

"Personally, I would love to take credit for blowing up the Enterprise—I've been wanting to do it for years! I always thought it would be an incredibly emotional visual moment if it were done properly. Of course, if the fans were really offended by the loss of the Enterprise, they could always postulate that Starfleet has a huge mothball fleet of similar ships and they could always reactivate another one." Perhaps reconsidering these rash words, Ralston went on to make the observation, "The Enterprise had character. Come to think of it, I don't know if the fans would ever accept any ship other than the Enterprise."

Even so, the Enterprise died in STAR TREK III, just as Spock had in STAR TREK II. Of course, the original Enterprise constructed for STAR TREK: THE MOTION PICTURE was not destroyed, any more than Leonard Nimoy was actually killed in THE WRATH OF KHAN. It, like Spock, would stage a resurrection in the very first STAR TREK film produced after its untimely demise.

Again, Ken Ralston described the effects he and his team created: "The whole ship blows up in a series of shots. The bridge goes, then the ship starts to keel over and—this is the shot I just had to get in—you see the famous NCC-1701 sapping away in a real close shot. Then the saucer comes up towards the camera, and the whole thing blows up in one big, fiery mass. Then there's a long shot of the Enterprise falling out, with most of the dome blown off and only the gridwork left. Then it falls into the planet. They have a few long shots of this comet going down, seen from the surface as Kirk and his people stand there, and he's saying, 'What have I done?' It's a good moment—very powerful."

For the shots involving the actual destruction of the Enterprise, ILM technician Ted Moehnke and his crew worked with partial models which were quickly destroyed and not with any of the actual Enterprise models employed in previous films. A new Enterprise model, one-third smaller than what was normally photographed, was built for full shots of the partially destroyed starship. In order to destroy the starship in an utterly convincing fashion, while maintaining the drama inherent in the scene, Moehnke and team started out with destroying the little dome on top of the saucer, replete with plenty of little explosions with cannons and balloons inside the ship. The explosions were timed carefully to give the entire sequence a rhythm that would heighten the sense that this was a truly immense space craft that was being torn apart in its death throes. The final explosion was photographed at 360 frames a second—with explosions timed to within three or four frames.

MELTING AWAY

ILM technician Don Dow recalled that the model built for the destruction sequence didn't require any extensive lighting or some of the other details usually used for models. The entire Enterprise bridge area had been completely blown away, so, quite logically, there were no more functioning lights remaining on board the dying ship.

For the desired effect of the skin melting away prior to the dome blowing up, the effects team constructed an additional saucer dome replica that was about six or eight feet in diameter, using a very thin styrene plastic for the shell, and then they shot it at a slow frame rate—a quarter of a second per frame—as they dropped acetone on the surface. (Quite simply, they stood over this model section and dripped acetone and other solvents onto the model out of squeeze bottles, while wearing proper eye protection and gas masks to avoid the fumes.) Of course, the acetone ate the plastic away, and when that was sped up to 24 frames per second, it really looks like a melting effect.

They actually sprayed the acetone on the outside while they were shooting. The problem they had was that they could see the drops on the first test—it looked like rain coming down. So they had to devise different methods of spraying the acetone on; and they employed different chemicals, as well. Other solvents would react with the plastic at different rates. A couple of places where they had decals for the ship identification numbers would not melt as fast as the other areas, so the timing here was a little bit tricky. Then they went in and did the fire effects, shooting again with the same program and the same frame rate.

To get the fire effects, the entire dome was laid over with steel wool which was lit in several areas at once to create burning pools in different areas. This resulted in a deep glow rather than actual flames, thereby creating the illusion of something burning in the vacuum of space.

In actual fact, steel wool itself does not burn; the fire was actually burning the oil that was *on* the steel wool; the steel itself was heated to a red glow but it was not burning, it was really melting. The only problem with this approach was that, as the steel wool melted under all this heat, a lot of little shards of molten steel would tend to fly off from the model under destruction. When these shards flew off, it was unavoidable that they would create an unwanted fireworks effect.

MORE DESTRUCTION

ILM's animation department had to go in and rotoscope every single spark out of the footage provided by Ralston. They tried to eliminate it as much as possible on the stage by using spray bottles filled with water to extinguish the embers as they came off the model. What they found which was even better, though, was just simply being a bit more careful about how they laid the steel wool out in the first place. The type of steel wool that they utilized for this effect was packaged in a pad which they simply unrolled; this provided them with a nice, flat, smooth piece of steel wool about six or twelve inches long. Once this was worked out, the effect came off without a hitch.

The interior shots of the destruction of the Enterprise were overseen by Paramount's special effects supervisor, Bob Dawson. He quickly encountered difficulties in blowing up the bridge, especially with regard to the elevator doors. These had been constructed out of Fiberglas, which is very hazardous to burn or explode with anyone around. Dawson scrapped the Fiberglas doors and reconstructed them with balsa wood. Behind these new doors, Dawson placed steel tubes, nine inches in diameter, and inside each of these he placed small bombs, some two ounces and some four ounces in weight, which were tamped into place with a packing agent that had been treated with gasoline.

Like the destruction of the Genesis set, which Dawson also oversaw, the demolition of the Enterprise sets could only be done once. Fortunately, the timing on all the explosions went off without a hitch. The pipes behind the doors served as mortars, propelling the bombs within them to nice effect. These, along with all the other charges set and detonated by Dawson's pyrotechnical crew, did a spectacular job in bringing an end to the Enterprise bridge set.

Dawson nearly met with disaster when he rigged the explosion of a corridor set. Apparently some of the charges had a bit too much gunpowder in them, and when Dawson, standing at the allegedly safe end of the hallway set, triggered the charges, a fireball rushed down the corridor, burning has face and arms. Dawson was rushed to the hospital, but, after several days of recuperation, a bandaged Dawson returned to continue and complete his work of THE SEARCH FOR SPOCK.

Matte painter Coroleen Green created a stunning matte painting for the final dramatic shot of the ruins of the Enterprise streaking across the sky of Genesis as Kirk and crew look on aghast from the troubled surface. The creatures that populated the Genesis planet were created by David Sosalla, who sculpted the rapidly-evolving worm creatures that posed such a problem to new visitors to Genesis. First came the smaller version. Sosalla's creature team made the worms from Hot-Melt, which is the same material squirmy toys are made from— a material that sets when heated to a certain temperature.

BURNING WORMS

They had to try and keep it clear too—they wanted a translucent feeling to everything, so they had to be careful about the temperature. The Hot-Melt tended to burn rather easily, and once it was burned, it turned brown. The worm builders were going through the worm molds fairly quickly, which was a bit of a problem because they were not set up for doing large batches of Hot-Melt. After they had assembled about a hundred or more of the worms that the scene required, they painted them, using a lot of a slimy, gooey substance known as methacyl.

Then the creature effects team ran fishlines all around the set, which were then run through a bunch of holes in the set. The worms themselves, were attached to the fishline. Then they tied the fishlines to rods underneath, and made some other little rods that would come up and poke at the worms. The idea was to make the worms move enough so that they would look alive, and also to avoid any dead spots in the worm-covered areas. Eventually they would have sometimes as many as ten or fifteen people under there pushing these rods up and down, pulling on fishline so that the worms would wriggle and write in an appropriately wormy fashion.

Unfortunately, these cute little slimeball critters evolved into larger, nastier monster worms, which would eventually give Klingon Commander Kruge (Christopher Lloyd) a bit of a tussle as he investigates the strange new world of the cataclysmically evolving Genesis planet. David Sosalla remembered them vividly, if not exactly fondly. "They're a bit like the Ceti eels from STAR TREK II. It was necessary to give some kind of motion to the front of them, to make them look meaner than just a wormy head. I came up with a system [of making the worms move] of making these long preshaped air bladders that I'd hook up to a series of quick-connect air hoses.

Sosalla goes on, "Then I could pile these things, have several switches for the air passages, and two people could push these little switches. one set of bags would fill and move into their predesignated shapes. Then you'd let the air out of those, and inject air into another set of bags, and other worms would undulate. They gave a real organic movement to the worms. And we'd have people off to the side pulling tail-end pieces through the shot, so that there would be some additional crawling and undulation. The visualization of the movement was exciting when you could stand back and play with it, but the final cut is so quick you never get the full impact." [CINEFEX, Aug. 1984]

SLIPPERY LITTLE BUGGERS

When the worms attacked Commander Kruge, Sosalla and crew had a problem on their hands. "There was so much slime on [the worms] that it would have shown in the shot when they reversed it. They didn't have the opportunity to do a number of takes because it would have ruined Kruge's makeup. So, they had to do it in real time. One cut shows a worm wrapping around Kruge's arm. For that, all they had to do was have the string [attached to the worm] going around his arm. Then two people in front would use their lines to pass it over. I was in back, and would grab my lines and pull. they had three people standing behind [Kruge]. Kirk Thatcher had one of the worm tales on his arm, and Nilo Rodis would feed the worm up [Christopher Lloyd's] back. One of the effects crew members and I had strings of our own going out in different directions. He would pull it far enough in one direction to get the worm whipping around, and as soon as it came over the back of Kruge's shoulder, I grabbed it and pulled, while Nilo kept feeding it."

Giant worms soon proved to be the least of Kruge's problems, of course, as he and Kirk eventually battle to the death against the apocalyptic backdrop of the death throes of the Genesis planet. The destruction of Genesis actually took place on Stage Fifteen of the Paramount lot, also known as the DeMille Stage in honor of its part in the filming of THE TEN COMMANDMENTS. Stage Fifteen stands as one of the biggest sound stages in Hollywood. The Genesis set, when completely constructed, measured three hundred by one hundred square feet, and contained a considerable variety of dramatic scenic backgrounds. Lush tropical jungles, freezing Arctic wastes and arid deserts all had to be represented there on that Paramount sound stage. The setting of the ultimate importance was to be the volcanic set where the final battle between Kirk and Kruge was staged while the surrounding terrain was wracked with seismic activity.

The Genesis planet also existed as a miniature set which preceded the construction of the various portions of the Stage Fifteen set; the miniature set itself was rather extensive and had to be cut up into smaller four-foot square sections. The miniature set had in fact been constructed to visualize in three dimensions the production sketches for the Genesis set, although it was also to be used for shooting various effects work as well. The miniature set sections also served as guidelines for the use of the studio carpenters in their construction of the Genesis sets. The miniatures were so complete that they even included scaled-down versions of the elaborate trussing systems which were designed to open up vast cracks in the ground of Genesis as the earthquakes grew in intensity. The carpenters were better able to visualize their task with the use of these miniature models, avoiding the errors that would have inevitably crept into a construction job derived entirely and directly from blueprints.

For the live-on-Stage Fifteen destruction of the Genesis planet, supervisor Robert Dawson employed a fourteen-man stage crew. Dawson had undertaken a similar earthquake sequence before when he had worked on the television miniseries SHOGUN, but the earthquakes for that program had not been anywhere near as intense or complex as those involved here for STAR TREK III: THE SEARCH FOR SPOCK. However, the basic techniques were essentially the same in both cases.

ONE LARGE SET

The Genesis set, as ultimately completed, was up to twenty-five feet in height. What Dawson required for the earthquake sequences was a number of fissures that opened up in the set. These needed to be anywhere between twenty and sixty feet in length, an average of four or five feet across, and about ten or twelve feet deep. To effect the fissures, the framework of the set was built on a raised wooden truss system. Beginning with a framework of four-by-four wooden beams, in rows divided by six-foot intervals, Dawson and his construction team then filled in the spaces with slightly inclined sheets of lumber.

The wooden cross beams supporting the set were partially sawed through in the middle, and had a hinge attached on to these pre-weakened sections. Cables were then attached to the weakened support beams. The entire area was filled in with sawdust and dirt and the set was constructed on top of this. Over a basic plywood base, the set construction team first layered gray slag from an old steel mine as the basic soil, mixed with decomposed granite, which was then covered with topsoil and various trees and other plants. When it came to the time where the fissures were required to appear in the set, the cables were pulled; the wooden supports gave way, the dirt and sawdust fell in quite convincingly, and a realistic looking crack in the ground was thus produced. William Shatner and other actors actually worked against these effects as they were being created live on the set, replete with various pyrotechnic effects.

For more peaceful, pre-destruction aspects of Genesis, a simple waterfall was built, using an old garden recycling pump which someone had discovered among a pile of disused props, and setting it up among a number of oversized fiberglass boulders that had probably first been used back in the early 'sixties. The unearthly quality of the water in the waterfall was created by the simple technique adding dry ice and food coloring to the water.

Returning to the destruction of the Genesis planet, however, part of the stage set was rigged for a variety of explosions by Robert Dawson. A mixture of naphthalene and propane gases known as nap-gas was used to create the jetting flames that came out of some of the earthquake fissures. Also involved were smoke effects, which utilized smoke canisters, and fog effects, which employed mineral oil. The final shooting of the destruction sequence— which had to be done perfectly on the first take— again used a fourteen-man crew, and again, wind machines and other noise producing equipment made it necessary for the crew to communicate with hand signals.

LEFT ON THE EDITING FLOOR

Once Kirk has defeated Kruge, it is time to get his friend Spock off of the rapidly self-destructing Genesis planet. One interesting and spectacular effect for this sequence was cut from the film. It depicts Kirk cradling the body of Spock amid vast cataclysmic upheavals, with an immense sun looming over the horizon. The idea, presumably, was that the Genesis planet was already careening on a collision course with its sun, but the scene was dropped mainly because it was implausible that Kirk and Spock could survive such an upheaval. At any rate, it was not entirely clear what exactly was happening in this effects shot. Still, the effect looked quite incredible. Too bad it was trimmed from the final cut.

Another Vulcan scene excised form STAR TREK III was production illustrator Tom Lay's design for the Vulcan Hall of Ancient Thoughts, a very sacred Vulcan site where the psychically reintegrated Spock would have been taken for part of his recovery rituals. This set, as designed by Lay, would have featured immense heads representing great philosophers and scientific thinkers of Vulcan history, twenty-foot tall sculptures illuminated by vast balls of fire. (Lay admitted that the heads were actually large photographic cutouts!) But because the scenes on Vulcan were deemed to take up too much screen time, this and other Vulcan sequences were trimmed from the final cut.

Soon enough, the entire film was assembled and released. Once again, Paramount Studios found themselves with a winner on their hands, thanks in no small part to the team at Industrial Light and Magic. Without ILM, they would certainly never have been able to bring Spock back to life, and destroy the Enterprise— and an entire planet— in the process. STAR TREK III: THE SEARCH FOR SPOCK was, without a doubt, a major special effects triumph, and one which suggested rather strongly to Paramount that it *probably* wouldn't be a bad idea to try it again.

The special effects demands for THE VOYAGE HOME were very different from the previous films. They needed to make mock-ups of whales look so real that audiences wouldn't notice that they were seeing special effects.

5

The Voyage Home

$\mathbb{S}$TAR TREK IV, directed, like its predecessor, by Leonard Nimoy, was to prove yet another rousing success for Paramount Studios— and for Industrial Light and Magic. Not only did Leonard Nimoy bat a thousand for Paramount again in his second directorial undertaking, he also spent as much time in front of the camera as behind it, truly performing this double duty with great aplomb. The fact that this was not an easy task to accomplish would be sadly demonstrated by the lesser film that would follow.

Although Nimoy did not script this outing, he did have considerable input with regards to the basic story idea for the movie. An initial script draft was completed in August 1985 by the writing team of Steve Meerson and Peter Krikes which involved a present-day character portrayed by Eddie Murphy. However, Murphy's attention wandered elsewhere well before the show got on the road.

The environmentally conscious Leonard Nimoy had come up with the notion that an environmental theme involving whales was what the story needed, and this was the thrust of the second screenplay, co-written by producer Harve Bennett and WRATH OF KHAN director Nicholas Meyer based on the initial drafts written by Steve Meerson and Peter Krikes.

The story involved a number of special effects even though its present-day setting obviated the need for the usual high incidence of effects and makeup work. Few new space craft models were required. The Bird of Prey would be obliged, among other things, to undergo the solar-slingshot time travel technique originally used on the classic STAR TREK television series of the sixties; later, it would crash into the waters beneath the Golden Gate Bridge right in the middle of a raging storm. Of course, there was also the pressing question of how to portray the all-important cetaceans on screen. The decision—not a difficult one, really—to stick with the tried and true effects house that had done such fine work on all but the first STAR TREK movie was reached with a minimum of fuss.

GETTING READY FOR BUSINESS

Nimoy and his STAR TREK IV production team first contacted George Lucas' Industrial Light and Magic in November of 1985. Heading the Industrial Light and Magic team were

Ken Ralston (visual effects supervisor) and Don Dow (director of effects photography). Design duties were shared by Industrial Light and Magic art director Nilo Rodis and visual consultant Ralph McQuarrie, well known for his work on George Lucas' STAR WARS movies. This time out, Industrial Light and Magic had their work cut out for them.

The first Industrial Light and Magic work to grace the film involved the Vulcan scene where the restored Spock rejoins his friends in the Bird of Prey and heads back to Earth. ILM's matte painting department, headed by Chris Evans, created this effect. It involved various foreground elements, primarily rocks, the miniature model of the Klingon Bird of Prey, a motion controlled sun, and Lieutenant Saavik and Spock's mother, bluescreened in against all the other elements. They were then all tied together in a sweeping panning motion. Chris Evans' matte painting team for the STAR TREK IV project consisted primarily of Randy Johnson, Don Dow, Wade Childers and Craig Barron on the cinematography end, and, in the painting department, Frank Ordaz, Sean Joyce and Evans himself.

For this film, they also created one of the most complicated matte shots that ILM has ever put together during its illustrious career: the exterior shot of Starfleet Command, complete with a space shuttle in the foreground and a latent image element which showed live actors interacting with the shuttle image as well as that of the Starfleet building! The live action sequence cheated a little; that footage wasn't filmed in San Francisco, really, but rather on an empty section of jet runway at Oakland Airport, on the other side of the bay. Here, actors dressed in Starfleet costuming had to follow meticulous blocking. Tape marks told them where they could and could not walk. On top of all this planning, the shadows of the objects planned for the matte were actually painted in silhouette on the concrete of the runway itself!

Industrial Light and Magic then found itself faced with the task of creating the crisis on Earth in Kirk's Twenty-third Century: a strange alien probe is wreaking havoc with Earth's ecosystem, causing violent global weather disasters. Because Starfleet is centered in San Francisco, the storms had to be shown pummeling the Golden Gate bridge. Jeff Mann of Industrial Light and Magic supervised the construction of a miniature Golden Gate Bridge model. This model would wind up being sixteen feet long, even though it would only represent half of the famed (and apparently long-standing) bridge. So, one tower alone of the bridge was shown. To further complicate matters, the model was constructed in forced perspective: the foreground section was sixteen inches wide while the other, background end was a mere two inches across! For the storm sequences, Mann and his underlings built an enclosed housing for the model, about a hundred square feet in area and twenty feet tall. The model was situated in a water tank and bombarded with every sort of storm effect that could be created live: rain, wind, smoke and clouds.

GOING TO ALL EXTREMES

These effects were composited against the windows of the Federation Council Chamber so that those inside it could appear to be witnessing the meteorological havoc occurring outside. An earlier attempt to film the actual Golden Gate Bridge during a storm produced some footage as well, but it was found that the real storm just did not look disastrous enough.

Mann and his team also worked on the alien probe which caused all this trouble. The logical idea was to have the probe resemble an earthly cetacean to some degree; for the first images of the entity that propels the plot of STAR TREK IV, Nilo Rodis basically conceptualized the mysterious space probe that triggers Earth's crisis as somehow resembling a whale itself. Mann and his team went so far as to paint the probe a light blue with white markings that suggested barnacles!

Recalled Mann: "Since Nilo's concept was that the probe looked similar to a whale, we built a prototype that was a cylinder shape with barnacles and whale-like coloring, but still basically just a tube. We capped the ends of a piece of irrigation pipe and installed a mechanism to turn the ball-like antenna that jutted out from the bottom. Our primary probe model was eight feet long, but we also made a small one for the long-distance shots and another big section that was a forced perspective model, about twenty feet long and really wide at one end and tapered back at the other. That was for a STAR WARS type shot of the probe coming over the heads of the audience, and it really made it look massive, as if it went on forever."

There was little need for Jeff Mann and his team to build any new spacecraft miniatures for STAR TREK IV; the story had little call for any. For the Saratoga in the opening sequences, Industrial Light and Magic simply put a new paint job on the Reliant model which Khan hijacked in STAR TREK II: THE WRATH OF KHAN. The shuttlecraft Grissom from THE SEARCH FOR SPOCK was resurrected as the Copernicus. The shuttle flown by Scotty in STAR TREK: THE MOTION PICTURE was also hauled out of mothballs and back into service with a new back added to the model.

Also finding its way into STAR TREK IV was the space dock model used in the previous film. Jeff Mann was impressed by the work that this entailed. Attempts to use stock footage of the space dock failed, making it necessary to shoot exclusively new footage. But all this was incidental to the area of primary concentration which involved Industrial Light and Magic this time around.

WANTING SOMETHING BETTER

The whales were crucial to the storyline. There was, in fact, only one live whale in the entire film. The shot in question was the surface shot at sea of a whale breaching which was shot for STAR TREK IV by photographers Mark and Debbie Ferrari. Every other whale shot in THE VOYAGE HOME was a miniature, articulated or mechanical reproduction of all or some portion of a whale's anatomy. Bennett observed that although there had been many whale pictures in the past, almost all of them suffered the minute that they put any variety of mechanical whales in the film.

The killer whale pictures (ORCA and others like it) got by because it is possible to train a killer whale to do things. Miniature effects were the problem that Bennett was afraid would be the THE VOYAGE HOME's week point. As it turned out, it was the easiest of his problems. He felt that Industrial Light and Magic provided, not only a simple, but a downright brilliant solution to the whale question. In fact, Bennett was certain that the only reason STAR TREK

IV did not win an Academy Award for its special effects was because the whales were so good that everyone in the audience was absolutely convinced they were real!

Industrial Light and Magic's Don Dow recalled his initial approach to the whale problem. The producers, according to him, knew that nothing else in the script was going to be a big problem, but he remembers that they were very anxious with regard as to how the ILM team was going to deal with the whale problem. In fact, they had alternate creatures in mind and were ready to change the script accordingly in case the whales never did work out.

It was just about that time that Humphrey the whale swam into San Francisco Bay— almost as if he had heard that STAR TREK needed whales for the latest film in the series and had come in to audition. The ILM team grabbed their cameras and spent several days chasing Humphrey up in the delta trying to photograph him. All they really intended to do was to get a little bit of reference footage, but director Leonard Nimoy became extremely excited about the possibility of getting some whale footage that he could actually use in the film.

Unfortunately, various difficulties precluded this possibility, including a certain camera-shyness observable in the famous wandering whale himself. Just about every time the camera crew got close enough to Humphrey the whale and got their cameras set up, the elusive whale would be off to a different spot, rendering it impossible to get any footage. It was ill advised to get in the water with him because he was an endangered species. But, the effects team *was* able to spend a lot of time observing the wayward whale, a fact that would help them immensely later in creating their whale effects.

ROBOTICS IS THE ANSWER

It was decided that robotics would probably work better than any utilization of optical processes; in other words, however they were done, the whales had to be filmed "live." To this end, Industrial Light and Magic contracted the services of robotics expert Walt Conti. Conti recalled that, to him, it was really quite ambitious to build something like this, totally self-contained and radio controlled. As far Conti was aware, there was absolutely no precedent for it.

Conti was convinced that art director Nilo Rodis thought that Conti could be talked into anything since he had no film experience and had no idea what could or could not be done! His biggest worry was whether he would really be able to control the mechanical whale effects. Although it was technically possible to make a whale move and flop around, would they make it actually go where they wanted it to go? As it turned out, that aspect of it wasn't the most critical.

Without much trouble they could hit a foot-square target across the pool in any direction. They had more problems in things like the materials, the skin wrinkling, and such. It was definitely the most efficient way to handle the whale sequences because they were able to avoid the optical process completely. They were fortunate in that the people behind the film—Harve Bennett, Ralph Winter and Leonard Nimoy—really cared about the quality of the whales. Rather than go the traditional route, they were willing to take the risk and finance the development of a totally new approach to underwater creatures. What Conti and the ILM team did on STAR TREK IV: THE VOYAGE HOME really opened up a whole new tool chest for directors. In fact, you can't help but wonder how much simpler Stephen Spielberg's JAWS might have been if it had been done with this kind of approach.

The script called for very specific moves and angles and lighting conditions that made some of the more traditional options unacceptable. For example, director Leonard Nimoy and the film's producers had initially looked at using real whale footage that had already been shot, but that would have been far too difficult to match that footage to the specific moves called for in the movie script. Also, there isn't much whale footage in existence in the thirty-five millimeter film format. So the seemingly easy stock-footage option was thrown out rather early on in the game, and Industrial Light and Magic inherited the problem of the whales.

SEARCHING FOR THE RIGHT EFFECT

Their first reaction to this challenge was to shoot a miniature against bluescreen and then composite it into some water plates. They found that it was extremely difficult to get any subtlety of movement and the right kind of light interaction. It could be done, but it would promise to be a very lengthy and unnecessarily complicated process. Another alternative was to shoot full-size mechanical whales on tracks—which was ultimately done for shots of the whales breaking the surface of the water. However, that approach limited them to very specific angles and movements and just didn't seem flexible enough for the underwater sequences.

In many ways, Conti's lack of film experience was an advantage on this project. However, Conti knew that it would be quite a challenge because it is obviously more difficult to replicate a real mammal than it is to do a fictitious creature. The movie audience knows, very specifically, how a real mammal moves. But Conti discovered that the movement could be simplified tremendously by keeping the front half of the whale rigid and having all the motion in the tail and in the pectoral fins.

They hurriedly put together a thirty-inch prototype to show to Paramount and to demonstrate their approach. This model had the required tail motion and was also free-swimming, but it still had an umbilical cord coming out of it for its power source. They threw that together and filmed it and showed the footage to Paramount, and the studio was quite impressed. The studio, predictably, immediately started nit-picking about barnacles and the paint job, but it was clearly obvious that Industrial Light and Magic was definitely on the right track. At that point, they were able to relax a little bit and they could proceed with the final design.

Peter Folkens, of the Oceanic Society, was called in to produce whale drawings for ILM's reference; Folkens utilized very specific animal data to proportion the animal. Folkens' meticulous attention to detail, and particularly in the musculature of the tail, turned out to be indispensable information for Conti and his collaborators. Richard Miller did the actual sculpting, with Folkens supervising very closely in order to insure accuracy. A four-foot whale was ultimately decided on, primarily because it was necessary to keep the model as small as possible in order to have room enough to fit in all the servos and radio gear. Four feet was also a very manageable proportion.

The effects team then spent a number of months doing research on finding the proper tail thickness for the mechanical miniature whale. This was a very important consideration because if the tail was built too thin it would buckle when it bent. If it was too thick, the electrical servos couldn't bend it. It took Conti and his crew six weeks to find just the right thickness for the tail alone.

MOVING ON

Once that question was resolved, they were ready to proceed with the rest of the whale model. The whale miniature ultimately consisted of a three-piece fiberglass exterior, but a problem arose: the delicate electro-mechanical devices in the whale were simply not very well adapted to functioning underwater. A lesson was learned the hard way: Servos and water just don't mix. Conti recounted how the problem was solved:

"We decided it was easier to seal each independent electrical servo rather than try to seal the entire whale. At twelve feet down, one little leak will kill you, so we decided to concentrate on what we wanted to keep dry and just let everything else get flooded. Each fin had to move independently up and down, fore and aft and rotate. It was pretty complex. The tail, however, was quite simple. It was just a universal joint pivot controlled by two electrical servos. It was a real simple hinge that moved up and down and side to side, and all the bending and arc-of-the-tail movement was achieved by the way the skin was shaped.

He continued, "The skin was made from a polyurethane manufactured by Smooth-On. In its normal state it's quite rigid so we had to add a lot of plasticizer to make it flexible enough. The most critical area was the tail. With most material, you shape it like a tail and bend it and you'll get wrinkles. That was especially a problem since we were working in miniature and those kind of wrinkles would ruin our scale. We tried a segmented tail with stretch skins over it—which is typically done with creature tails—but that just wasn't working at all. Finally, we tried a really thick polyurethane skin cast in a tube and it was perfect. When we pulled it out of the mold it felt just like blubber. So we ended up with a really thick tail, about an inch to an inch-and-a-half thick all the way around. Then we had a thinner front half of the whale—about a quarter-inch [thick] from the mid-point forward—to allow room for the mechanics. We had to cast some inserts into the flippers and the flukes to make them stiff enough to resist the water and yet flexible enough that you could see some kind of deflection. It took some experimenting to find that balance. We ended up putting spring steel into the actual mold and then casting rubber around it. That gave us quite a nice, graceful movement."

ADDING DETAILS

Microballoons were added to the skin to get the buoyancy they needed to make the whales actually appear to swim. Conti and his cohorts also balanced this buoyancy by positioning some lead weights inside to the whale to make it horizontally correct. The whale model had to sit in the water just right in order for the robotics expert to control it effectively.

Conti and his team also built a water pump into the model; this pump had a water intake right underneath the chin of the whale. Fortunately, whales have a patch of barnacles on their chins, so it was a matter of the utmost simplicity for Conti to disguise the pump using barnacles. The water pump was employed to actually turn the whale. Simply by turning the tail to one side and then activating the pump, it was possible to make whale turn just like a jet boat. The pump also enabled it to dive down or come up in the water. Although Conti had, prior to this, been concerned that he would need the pump to make it go forward too, it turned out that the robotic whale copied the swimming action of a real whale so well that it had absolutely no need of any additional mechanical assistance.

Conti's team, with cameraman Pete Romano, filmed the underwater sequences in the pool at a nearby high school! Romano, a real trooper, would often spend the entire day in the swimming pool, enduring considerable cold most of the time. Despite his discomfort, he stuck it out with a stoical reserve until the filming was completed. Conti and Romano discovered that the most dramatic lighting effects could be obtained later in the evening when the sun started to set. Shafts of light from the setting sun provided a greater sense of perceptual depth for the underwater footage, as the light tended to diffract in the chlorinated water of the pool.

In addition to four "whale wranglers"—two above water and two below—there was need for additional help. A couple of divers with video assist cameras were soon brought in to help Romano and Conti observe the relationship between the cameraman and the whales. These monitors did not solve everything; even *with* the monitors it was rather difficult for the filmmakers to see what they were doing. For example, it was necessary for them to muddy up the water pool with diatomaceous earth in order to simulate ocean water, as well as to create the required sense of scale. If someone was out in the ocean and encountered a forty-foot whale, they would discover that while the whale's head would be very clear to see, the tail of the cetacean would be less distinct.

HARD OF HEARING

In order to realize that same effect on a four-foot model, they found that they needed to have a bit of cloudiness in the water. Further complicating the shoot were the constantly blowing wind machines which were used to create the stormy effects of the ocean surface. The wind machines compromised the operators' ability to see. Conti and his team had made the mechanical whale models extremely maneuverable, and in a clear pool they were more than able to achieve just about anything with them, but when it came time to shoot the final whale effects footage, they had difficulties which were, unfortunately, inherent in the need to cloud the waters for the sake of realism.

To get around this, Romano learned to be very careful, and to photograph the mechanical whales only at certain angles. Technically, shooting the whales swimming from underneath was *the* optimal angle for filming them because it made them look so much larger. But most people are simply not accustomed to seeing a whale from that position. Audiences are accustomed to seeing these animals photographed from specific angles, and if the cinematographers were to deviate too much from the commonplace, their efforts simply would not appear realistic.

One shot that gave Conti especially hard time was the sequence where the whales turn to a vertical position to sing their response to the probe. It was very difficult for Conti and his crew to get them into a vertical position and stop there, all in one cut. Eventually they found it more effective to "cheat" a little bit. They utilized some monofilament to pull the noses of the mechanical whale models down into the position required.

Conti and his effects team were very excited about doing the scene with the whales breaching alongside the crashed Klingon Bird of Prey. Their first approach was to actually breach the miniature out of water with jets of air shooting around it to break up the water molecules. When that didn't work they switched over to a "dry" approach where the whale was positioned underneath a thin membrane that had had sugar and flour piled up on top of it. The idea behind this was to film the effect with a miniature water tank in front of it and have the whale shooting out behind the tank.

They drove the whale upwards with a spring-loaded catapult, which would make the whale break through the membrane and throw all the dry materials up into the air. To accommodate the fact that whales also turn over onto their backs when they breach, the rig had a rotation on it. This setup was really somewhat crude at this point in the testing. Conti and his team were just using prototypes, but despite its shortcomings, this setup allowed them to test out materials and the basic concept. The tests looked very promising at this stage. Unfortunately, the producers decided not to go ahead with it—both for story and budgetary reasons—and they ended up just using some research footage that was shot for them in Hawaii. Conti's tests proved, to his mind, just how much better the dry approach appeared when dealing with miniatures. From a distance it looked just like spraying salt water.

HOMEWORK PAYS OFF

Rather than use opticals for scenes in which humans interact with the cetaceans, it was decided to use full, one-to-one scale whale sections. These were done at Paramount by Michael Lantieri and Robert Spurlock. Spurlock described some of these whale sections in a 1987 interview with CINEFEX magazine. "The tail, or fluke, was the most critical of the sections; it was about twelve feet wide and seventeen to eighteen feet long. Larry DeUnger and I spent two to three weeks going over pictures and books and videos of whales swimming and diving to try and home in on the movement of the fluke as it comes in and out of the water. We did all our tests with quarter scale sticks and paper mounted on layout board to try out the necessary mechanisms and to get the movement that Leonard wanted."

When the whale "waves" to the crew of the Enterprise, a ten-foot long fin was employed. Explained Lantieri, "In reality, I think that [waving] movement is to show anger, but Leonard wanted it as a sign of affection and to show the grace with which the whales could move. Then we had another section which was the blow-hole. That was employed mainly for scenes at the Cetacean Institute. You'd see flaring nostrils come up, there'd be a blow of air and water and then it would go back underwater. Finally we had a male and female back section, connected side by side, for the farewell shot at the end of the show.

Together these sections were integrated into the movie so as to convince the audience that there was an entire whale there. From the beginning, our biggest worry was having enough whale for each particular shot. We had arrived at these four pieces basically by studying the storyboards, and I told Leonard [Nimoy] that he was not going to be able to deviate from those boards too much without its creating a major change in what we were doing. Once he was pinned down to specific shots and angles, we knew that we could make our whale fit the storyboard and do what he wanted it to do.

"We were a little understaffed at Paramount, so we had the [whale] skins made off the lot by Lance Anderson and his shop. After they layered the skins up, Tom Pahk and Robin Reilly went over to help fit them. Any part of the whale that was going to have to bend was reinforced with Danskin leotard material and foam rubber so that the skin wouldn't tear. We then brought the skins back to Paramount and applied them over our Fiberglas shells."

Originally, they were going to go up north to a Sea World type place in Vallejo and shoot in a deep tank there, but it wasn't ready when they required it. "So we ended up in a four foot deep tank at Paramount. That required some drastic changes for us because the whale itself was six feet high. To get around that problem, we had to dig a hole in the bottom of the tank—twenty by forty feet across and six feet deep—to allow the fluke to dive completely underwater. Even at that, the tail just barely cleared the surface by six inches. Whenever we did a dive, we had to keep it pulled way down so it wouldn't pop back up into the shot."

NO ROOM FOR ERROR

Four hundred feet of steel track was involved in working the whale in the tank. Recalls Robert Spurlock, in a CINEFEX interview: "We couldn't have the track fail in any way, because under four feet of water it would have been very difficult to go back in and fix it. The fluke, the pectoral fin and the blowhole were all on dollies that were pulled through the shot by air motors. Specifically to get the shots of the fluke coming up and then diving back down underwater, there were two small humps in the track just before it ran down into the deeper tank.

Spurlock goes on, "The fluke was powered by two sets of hydraulics. there were two sets of cylinders—one set which pumped the whale and a second set that moved the fluke. All of the movement for its dive had to be choreographed between Al Rifkin, Larry DeUnger, Bobby Johnston and me. Bobby would pull the whale with one air winch. Then, once it went over the hump, Larry and I would add the coordinating fluke movement by operating the joysticks that controlled those hydraulics. Finally, Al would have to hit a brake in his air motor to slow it down as it went into the hole, which was very important since this thing weighed almost two thousand pounds."

Spurlock recalled the final whale section, a full-scale whale head employed in the scene where Spock mind-melds with Gracie, the pregnant cetacean. "The head had an eye piece built by Stuart Ziff that was cable actuated and moved up and down and back and forth. It also had a small pectoral fin that moved. We took the headpiece to a facility at McDonnell-Douglass where they have a big glassed-in tank that they use to simulate weightlessness for astronauts. The head was hung from very fine wires and then moved across the water with Leonard holding onto it doing his mind-meld. We also floated it a little bit by putting inner tubes inside to give it neutral buoyancy. Since the pectoral fin on one side created a weight, we added an outrigger on the other side to balance it— just a milk crate on the end of a pole with some counterweights. This was the only whale section that floated at all. Since all the others were mounted on tracks, it wasn't necessary for them to be buoyant."

When Kirk, Spock and crew, in the cloaked Bird of Prey, pursue the whale (the same model doubled for both the male and female whales) it must rescue Gracie from a whaling boat. Jeff Mann was assigned a rather unusual assignment. He had to take a full-sized boat and fit it to look like a whaling ship. They located a former World War II minesweeper, a forty-foot vessel named The Golden Gate; an additional bridge was added to the boat, as well as a harpoon deck. The harpoon gun, which fires at Gracie the whale only to have its harpoon bounce, crumpled, off the hull of the invisible spacecraft, was built by the Industrial Light and Magic pyrotechnics team along with the harpoons and assorted whale hunting materials.

LIVE FILMING

Once the Bird of Prey, with Gracie the whale on board, executes the slingshot time travel effect again and returns to the Twenty-third Century, it crashes into San Francisco bay right beneath the Golden Gate Bridge. This was filmed in the enclosed miniature weather set. Not only this, but everything in it was filmed live, including the Bird of Prey, which, in the sequence as filmed, was crashed "live" using a wire rig. For this sequence, Jeff Mann's team built four additional Bird of Prey models.

The Bird of Prey model used for motion control shots such as the time travel sequence was too expensive (not to mention reusable) to be utilized in the crash sequence. Mann and his team tried a number of "live" crash effects in the water tank before settling on the wire: their four models were set afire, suffered generally rough treatment, and were even, during the trial and error period, literally thrown into the water. Mann would actually take a model, hold it over his head and let it fly! Or, rather, let it crash into the eighteen inches of water in front of the forced-perspective Golden Gate Bridge miniature.

STAR TREK IV: THE VOYAGE HOME concluded with the inspiring revelation of the new Enterprise-A. What Kirk and his cohorts failed to realize (don't nobody tell them, now) was that this was, once again, the same old Enterprise that saw its first duty back in Douglas Trumbull's hands, in STAR TREK: THE MOTION PICTURE. The model showed all the wear and tear it had been through in its eight years of existence. Considerable repair work went into bringing the old special effects warhorse back into shape. After that monumental undertaking it was given a meticulous paint and detailing job that took nearly two months to complete.

In addition to providing the usual battery of new effects, STAR TREK IV: THE VOYAGE home also did some interesting work with the already-established STAR TREK special effects vocabulary. The most interesting was a first for STAR TREK: the first moving Transporter effect. In the sequence in question, Spock, is seen walking towards the camera, and is beamed up as he is in motion! The Transporter effect had to be motion controlled to match Nimoy's movement. The meticulous work on this shot, which some people didn't even notice, included having the Transporter effect "sparkles" fade out in conjunction with the movements of Spock.

Once again, thanks to ILM, Paramount's STAR WARS film series continued to undo the damage done by STAR TREK: THE MOTION PICTURE. In conjunction with the humanistic and environmentally correct script provided by Nicholas Meyer and Harve Bennett, the effects in STAR TREK IV: THE VOYAGE home truly brought this, perhaps the most pleasantly entertaining entry in the series, to vivid life on theater screens the world around. Things were going right for STAR TREK. Unfortunately, Industrial Light and Magic would not be around to pull Paramount's bacon out of the fire when a certain ham-turned-unproved-director took his turn at piloting the starship Enterprise from *behind* the camera.

In the fifth STAR TREK movie, William Shatner did it his way, with decidedly mixed results. A slashed special effects budget added to the film's problems.

6

The Final Frontier

Q: How many ears does Mister Spock have?

A: Three. A left ear, a right ear— and a final, front ear.

The most notable change in the special effects for this installment STAR TREK was the absence of Industrial Light and Magic. Prior commitments, such as GHOSTBUSTERS II, kept them from being involved. This was only one of many problems assailing executive producer Ralph Winters: the Writer's Guild strike of early 1988 delayed startup of the production, which in turn led to another prolonged wait while Leonard Nimoy completed the final cut of his drama THE GOOD MOTHER starring Diane Keaton. On top of this, both Nimoy and Shatner required a certain amount of persuasion to ensure their participation on screen.

The film's thirty-two million dollar budget dropped to twenty million after six million dollars apiece went to the two lead actors. This dwindling amount dropped even further after the other actors received their salaries and William Shatner received a second salary for his first outing as the director. Another factor in this film's troubled history was that the special effects had to be completed in three months (at best, half of the time usually required for a major science fiction film project) in order to meet Paramount's iron-clad release date.

To keep these matters from getting out of hand, Ralph Winter decided to avoid, as much as possible, the use of post-production optical effects, but rather to create as many of the effects as he could live on the set or through camera tricks while shooting. The destruction of the Genesis planet inside a sound stage in STAR TREK III: THE SEARCH FOR SPOCK was a fine example of 'live' special effects. Although even that sequence underwent quite a bit of opticals treatment after the completion of shooting.

After long consideration, Ralph Winter chose a visual effects team headed by Bran Ferren. Ferren's New York-based effects company, Associates and Ferren, had worked on such films as ALTERED STATES, THE MANHATTAN PROJECT, MAKING MR. RIGHT and the musical version of LITTLE SHOP OF HORRORS. With the decision to employ Bran Ferren's team, production of STAR TREK V became effectively divided between opposite sides of the continental United States. This exacerbated the difficulties inherent in dealing with the three-month special effects deadline. To make matters worse, communications problems frequently arose between Bran Ferren and neophyte director William Shatner. Shatner did not always seem to comprehend what Ferren was trying to do for the film and, conversely, often made demands (requests?) that demonstrated his lack of understanding of what special effects could or could not do.

UNFORESEEN DIFFICULTIES

The prologue of THE FINAL FRONTIER, which introduces the character of Sybok (Lawrence Luckinbill), involved having Sybok ride through a cloud of smoke, directly towards the audience. There were unforeseen difficulties with this seemingly simple scene: the original effects plan had been to strap a smoke canister to actor Luckinbill's back as he approached the camera on horseback, a simple technique that theoretically should have produced the desired effect. However, the smoke emitting from the canister simply trailed listlessly behind the actor! The dust cloud was abandoned, as well as the notion of having Sybok's cape wired with a rig which made it stand out behind him as if windblown.

The opening sequences of Kirk and Spock at Yosemite National Park were primarily accomplished using stunt doubles. Shots of Kirk on the rock face were filmed at a safe, railed-in view point, but with the railing and walkway concealed by a false rock facade. Local swimming pool owners obligingly allowed their pools to be covered over. (Apparently, swimming has become outmoded by the advent of the twenty-third century.) This was the only shot where Shatner was actually suspended at a high altitude; it was, however, necessary to get at least one establishing shot to show him high above ground level.

This three-thousand foot high shot took place on Glacier Point, a spot with a panoramic view of the Yosemite Valley. This was a potentially dangerous shot which some tried to talk the director out of, but he insisted. Of course, the cable which secured him to the mountain was capable of holding eight tons, which was certainly adequate to keep even William Shatner firmly in place, despite his weighty ego.

A key portion of this scene involved Kirk loosening some pebbles, which plummet downwards, emphasizing what Spock wryly referred to as "the gravity of [his] situation." It was inappropriate to send real rocks over the edge, since this would have been a danger to any climbers or campers below, so they employed foam pebbles which were tied together so that they could be recovered easily.

Spock's rocket boot-assisted "levitation" was largely accomplished by suspending him from a crane arm and shooting him and Shatner from the midsection up. Kirk's fall off the rock face of El Capitan was performed by stuntman Ken Bates who, in his safety rig, also managed to set the American distance record for such a fall. Close-ups of Shatner and Nimoy were shot at Paramount and optically composited using bluescreen techniques by Pacific Title.

OUT WITH THE OLD, IN WITH THE NEW

Gone was Shatner's original concept of showing Kirk on the face of El Capitan, with the camera starting in close-up of him clinging to the rock and then slowly zooming backwards until the entire Yosemite area was visible. This shot would have cost three hundred fifty thousand dollars. Shatner was actually filmed against a Fiberglas recreation of the wall of El Capitan, painted by Jimmy Betts to match the tones of the actual terrain, which was situated on the Paramount lot. Hidden hand holds enabled Shatner to keep a grip on things while he performed his dialogue. Some shots of the Fiberglas wall had to be redone, as it looked too shiny in some of the dailies, much to Shatner's dismay.

Nimoy's flying rig was actually a mold of his body. It was fabricated of Fiberglas and covered his body from thighs to chest. A pipe attached to the middle of this rig was attached to the false rock face on the Paramount lot. When Nimoy donned the body cast and attached to the wall, he appeared to be suspended in space some feet away from the wall, parallel with the rock-hugging (or Fiberglass-hugging) Shatner. For the flying sequence where Spock rescues Kirk, Nimoy wore a different rig. It was a metal bar attached at his waist, which literally flipped Nimoy head-over-heels to create his abrupt turnabout in pursuit of the plummeting Kirk.

For more difficult stunts, Nimoy was doubled by Greg Barnett. The middle section of Nimoy's "fall" was actually Barnett standing in for him, taking a dive off the Fiberglas El Capitan set and landing on a strategically placed air bag. (William Shatner's stunt double for STAR TREK V would be Donny Pulford, who had long served Shatner in the same capacity on the T.J. HOOKER series; DeForest Kelley was doubled by stunt man Tom Huff.)

Due to budgetary limitations and the tightly restricted production time allotted to STAR TREK V: THE FINAL FRONTIER, both producer Ralph Winter and his Bran Ferren preferred to avoid bluescreen and other optical effects as much as possible. This was especially important in the case of viewscreens on the live-action set. Ferren was determined to do as many of the viewscreen effects "live" as was possible. This was accomplished by actually setting up rear screen projection on the set where the viewscreen shots were to take place. Various starfield footage was then projected while the actors did their scenes in front of the screens.

ONCE AGAIN, MONEY TALKS

The film's first shot of the Enterprise provided some problems. The plan was to have the Enterprise fly past Earth's moon as Kirk and Spock shuttle up to the ship. Ferren's team felt that the Enterprise would appear in silhouette in the moonlight. Ralph Winter and others at Paramount felt that the Enterprise simply had to be lit in detail. They failed to understand that there was no light source between the Earth and the moon to produce such an effect. However, money talks, and numerous silhouette effects were scrapped in favor of what Paramount wanted. Their next effort, of a well-lit Enterprise suspended in stillness before the moon, was also scrapped when William Shatner commented that it looked like a piece of paper stuck onto the moon; another, moving shot was executed, and apparently everyone on the West Coast was satisfied with the result.

In order to get the bulk of the basic model photography done on time, Bran Ferren teamed up with Peter Wallach of Peter Wallach Enterprises, who had worked with Ferren's team on LITTLE SHOP OF HORRORS. Ferren and Wallach set out to find studio space large enough to do the requisite motion-control work, which seemed an impossible task—until they gained access to an out-of-service licorice factory in Hoboken, New Jersey. (Licorice enthusiasts will note that it was a Twizzlers facility that had specialized in the production of red licorice.) Vast quantities of equipment, including an entire machine shop, were moved into the licorice factory, and work began.

The most complicated effects sequence in STAR TREK V involved the crash of the shuttlecraft Galileo in the Enterprise shuttle bay. In this scene, Kirk and the shuttlecraft must get to the Enterprise before the Klingons attack. The Enterprise must lower its shields, but Kirk decides to minimize the shields down time by forgoing the use of a tractor beam to guide the shuttlecraft safely in to dock. Obliged to pilot the shuttle manually, Sulu manages a high speed crash landing, and escapes the Klingon attack.

In keeping with the requirement of doing effects "live," the team decided to literally launch the shuttlecraft model into the shuttle bay model at high speed! Because explosion effects would illuminate any sort of suspension rig, wires were out of consideration. Ferren was determined to stage a real crash. Peter Wallach devised a rig involving a sled and two large garage door springs, which was what they finally went with. After making various tests with plywood models— six in all— it was decided to go for the final shoot.

Pyrotechnics for the crash simulation were timed by a computer firing chip that was triggered photoelectrically and set off the sequence of twelve explosions that accompanied the crash. This allowed them to avoid the use of any external wires to trigger the explosions. Everything was actually contained within the shuttlecraft model. Everything, that is, except the trigger mechanism for the explosion which was to crack the thrusters on the shuttlecraft. For this, a circuit was rigged with a piece of plastic attached to a monofilament wire which led out of the model. When the catapulted model reached the point in its trajectory that was beyond the length of the wire, the plastic simply pulled out and closed the circuit, triggering the explosion.

OLD TRICKS

After Kirk's crew is safely back on board the Enterprise, they evade the pursuit of the murderous Klingon Bird of Prey by Zapping into high warp. The visual effects created here by Peter Wallach essentially reprised the basic techniques devised by Douglas Trumbull for STAR TREK: THE MOTION PICTURE. Trumbull's team had found that their motion control computer could not effectively "streak" the Enterprise model onto film. This situation forced them to do the shots by hand, moving the camera down its track on notch at a time.

Wallach's team did basically the same. Bob Lyons, stopwatch in one hand and a flashlight as light source in the other, timed each ten-second exposure. With the streaking being done for each single frame, this was a time-consuming process . Some streaks took as many as fourteen hours to produce. The entire sequence would have been even more difficult if the effects team didn't devise a manually operated capping shutter switch.

When Sybok talked the Enterprise crew into joining him on his God-quest to Sha Ka Ree, it became necessary to devise the special effects for the Great Barrier. The script described a rather daunting effect. This challenge was approached from a number of angles during the course of STAR TREK V's production, as the effects team struggled with the realization of this crucial effects sequence.

Bran Ferren's first approach to this challenge centered around tests involving ultraviolet water dyes. This provided the pulsating, cloudlike effect desired, but Paramount felt that the effect was too violent Although later, Paramount added lighting and other dramatic effects to the sequence.

The atmosphere of Sha Ka Ree was another ultraviolet effect. Rings of clear Plexiglas, nestled one within the other, were placed in a water tank and spun. This created a variety of spiraling currents which, when injected with ultraviolet dyes and shot with ultraviolet light, created the cloud effects required. This was shot with a snorkel lens inside the tank, using motion control, to provide the sensation of the ship passing through the churning clouds. The dyes involved were actually completely transparent to regular light.

OPTICALS PLAY AN IMPORTANT ROLE

The planet was also created from these effects. The effects shots translated into mattes to be composited against a starfield. The atmosphere itself was to be further complicated by thunderclouds with glowing lighting effects pulsing deep within them. The optical house did the work here: attaching some balls of cotton to a large flat piece of Plexiglas, they shot the 'clouds' from below with a rented thirty-five millimeter Arriflex camera. They shot the cotton balls deliberately out of focus, with the light source above the Plexiglas; variations in the intensity of the lighting provided the heat lightning effect. The Great Barrier effect, when ultimately composited, involved ultraviolet swirls, animated lighting blasts, the Enterprise, and various miscellaneous lighting effects.

When the Enterprise actually flies low and close to the surface of Sha Ka Ree, Bran Ferren attempted to recreate the look of the Trona Peaks, California terrain where the location live-action footage was filmed.

Originally Illusion Arts had been scheduled to create this sequence. It involved a considerably less uninviting world of Sha Ka Ree, using miniatures and paintings in combination. Shatner had recently been impressed by a retrospective exhibit of such Nineteenth Century American landscape painters as Frederic Church, Albert Bierstadt and Thomas Cole. Shatner had hoped to recreate their lush approach on the world of Sha Ka Ree. However the incredible shrinking budget made this impossible, and Sha Ka Ree became a desert world. The live action footage was shot in the desert. Syd Dutton and Illusion Arts bowed out, leaving the God Planet sequence in the capable hands of Bran Ferren.

For the rocky, desert-like effect desired, the redoubtable Ferren ultimately went for miniature effects—and *extremely* miniature effects at that! Ferren created a new piece of equipment for this undertaking: its basic element was a digital scanning electron microscope manufactured by the Zeiss optical works, which Ferren actually altered so that it could do motion control. This was combined with a four-thousand line digital image processing system and high-resolution scanners which transferred the images directly to the film stock. The video images were shot at a highly compacted resolution: two thousand and five hundred lines of resolution, to be exact, putting even Japanese high resolution television to shame.

Ferren then tested a number of microscopic textures to represent the planet surface. Pollen, sand, and various minerals were tested. In a burst of culinary inspiration, Ferren saved a lobster claw from his lunch, scanned it with the microscope, and found his terrain! (Ferren may seem to have been living high, with lobster lunches, but this pales when you consider that objects to be scanned with an electron microscope must be coated with a specific element in order to dispel electrical charges which can disrupt the imaging process. Before Ferren could even begin to test his leftovers, that lobster claw had to be plated with gold!)

For the live effects of Sha Ka Ree, Kirk and crew must find themselves in the midst of bizarre and violent seismic activities: Immense shafts of rock burst from the ground beneath their feet and create a church-like structure, from which the voice of "God" emanates, addressing them. On the Paramount set, stone shafts were constructed on the lot and filmed with a vertically moving camera to create the illusion of movement. In New Jersey, Ferren's team did the miniature version of the sequence.

TABACCO REALY SMOKES

The effect was designed by Mike Tabacco with additional design modifications created by Eric Moore and David Mei. The sequence took two months to shoot. The rock formation was lifted through the top of the effects table on top of an elevator device, which ran on rollerskate wheels over tracks, and which was raised through the use of counterweights. To assure multiple takes, the miniature planet surface was cast in plaster, and multiple casts were made as need required.

The effect was filmed at high speeds ranging from seventy-two to ninety-six frames per second. To create a satisfactory visual image, tests were made on the plaster employed to create the miniature terrain. Ultimately, Arnie Jacobsen and Jim Bock, the special effects engineers for the rockburst effect, mixed charcoal with the plaster to create the effect of geological layers being shattered as elevator-propelled shafts of stone shattered the plaster landscape on their way through to the surface. For the portions of the terrain not directly involved in the breakthrough effect, Joe Beymer covered carpeting with plaster.

When "God," portrayed by George Murdoch, tampers with the god-images of the various characters assembled, Paramount originally planned to use makeup effects, Various god-heads (pun intended) were sculpted by makeup prosthetics artist Kenny Myers. His creations included the Greek goddess Hera, an Andorian deity, a Klingon god, and various others, including George Murdock's own classic god image, beard, robes, and all. This last one actually owed its inspiration to the makeup and costume worn by Charlton Heston as Moses in Cecil B. DeMille's THE TEN COMMANDMENTS. The various deities looked too hokey when worn by actors, so the footage of them was sent East to Ferren for optical work. As completed, each head, in varying degrees of transparency, appeared out of a shining red globe (another water-tank effect) and ultimately became George Murdock's face.

The final appearance of Murdock-as-"God" was the result of considerable efforts by Bran Ferren. He tried, among other things, various computer imaging techniques, as well as solarization and other effects. Finally, Shatner and the producers decided to refer back to THE TEN COMMANDMENTS again; that film had simply employed light effects to represent Jehovah. A simple beam of light emerging from the planet, with the face of George Murdock in it, was the effect they decreed was required. They also wanted it done as an in-camera effect to avoid post-production delays that might slow the film's release date, which, like the ten commandments, was written indelibly in stone.

PULLING OUT ALL THE STOPS

The techniques devised by Ferren and his crew involved spinning cylinders, fifteen feet high and four feet around, which they wrapped in a wrinkled reflective plastic surface. The face of "God" was projected onto these, rendered hazy and more supernatural by a fog filter on the projectors employed in the sequence. Beam-splitting techniques were employed to match this effect with the live-action footage. During the live-action shoot the effect was enhanced by the use of a specially constructed rotating light drum which put out a searing twenty-thousand watts of light from a xenon source.

Shutters on this device added a pulsating effect which went with the effects footage created back East in Ferren's New Jersey studio. All this was very well and good, as might be imagined, but Paramount threw a wrench into the works and decided that they didn't want the face of George Murdock used in this effect to look as realistic as it did. Everything was scrapped, and, (surprise!) the sequence wound up being done as a post-production optical effect after all. The same cylinders were used by themselves as the element for the glowing light of "God" but the revised Murdock face shots were combined with this optically this time around.

Matters got weirder once the evil duplicate Sybok appears; In the original script the two Sybok's battle and implode, leaving a gaping hell-hole from which the residual essence of the evil false deity emerges. The original idea here— Shatner's— was to have the "God" character, accompanied by cherubim, toss Kirk, Spock and McCoy into "hell," with the attendant angels transforming into tormenting demons. However, this would have entailed creating latex suits for the stunt men who would wear them— suits which would have cost in the general vicinity of sixty thousand dollars a piece.

Ultimately, one rock man was all that survived by the time the film was completed. In a telling quote, Shatner commented: ". . .I had. . . the realization that the movie in my head was going to be different from the one in reality." Ferren worked hard to make the rockman effect created by Kenny Myers work, but he knew that making a rubber suit look like anything other than a rubber suit is one of special effect's greatest challenges. They even tried shooting the rockman suit at night (which has the residual effect in the film of it being daylight when Sybok confronts the entity nut night-time when Kirk and the others run back to the shuttlecraft). Ultimately the idea was scrapped; instead, the residual "god" energy became a simple ball of light which pursues Kirk until Spock, in a pirated Klingon Bird of Prey, destroys the entity with a phaser blast.

PAIN IN THE ASTEROID

For this final mountaintop scene, William Shatner was photographed on yet another piece of Fiberglas rock at the Paramount lot. No sooner had The Optical House's Bob Rowohlt completed his final compositing than Paramount called him to inform him that the sky in the shot was supposed to be black but had, instead, been turning out various shades of gray. The Optical House traced the problem to some mismatched film stock and corrected the problem by building up contrast. This was a useless endeavor, since Paramount changed film stocks again, which made it necessary to reshoot the Bird of Prey elements.

This whole sequence became a living hell for the technical crew photographing it. Robert Lyons programmed the new motion control movements for the Bird of Prey reshoot, only to have the motion control computer crash. To worsen matters, the monitor went on the fritz, so they could no longer see what it was that they were doing. With a week to go on the post-production deadline, they had to brazen it through. At last, the Bird of Prey was successfully refilmed and composited once more.

End of story? Not quite. When Paramount screened the scene they discovered something that the red lighting had blinded Andrew Laszlo to. It seemed that a member of the crew, apparently entranced by William Shatner's histrionic brilliance, had been sitting partially concealed, in a crack in the fiberglass mountaintop set. This was painfully visible when the film was projected on a screen. Robert Rowohlt corrected the problem with a matte, finally bringing this difficult sequence to its conclusion.

The Bird of Prey model in this film was the work of Greg Jein's model shop. Jein had built models for the other STAR TREK films and his crew's detail work on the Klingon Bird of Prey was one of the few high points of the special effects work in this film. Jein's shop was also responsible for building props for the film, but the prop budget was incredibly low, apparently the smallest of any of the films. This was surprising in light of the fact that STAR TREK IV: THE VOYAGE HOME had returned the greatest profit of any of the STAR TREK films to date.

Paramount was apparently still sore over the huge expenditure they made back in 1978 & 79 for STAR TREK—THE MOTION PICTURE. The reported $40 million budget for ST—TMP was inflated a bit when you consider that it didn't just include money spent on making that film. It also covered the money Paramount spent on its previous efforts to revive STAR TREK. This included expenditures for the aborted STAR TREK II television series and contracts with actors that had to be paid off when the project was canceled. But STAR TREK had gone on to prove itself a continuing money-making enterprise, which made the stinginess on the budget of THE FINAL FRONTIER that much more surprising. The mixed results and depressed box office showing was clearly as much Paramount's fault as anyone's.

SCENES THAT DIDN'T MAKE IT

Some scenes originally planned for STAR TREK V never made it to the final cut. Originally, Kirk and Spock's "vacation" sequence was to have been intercut with another sequence involving Sulu and Chekov, hiking in the Mount Rushmore area, although Yosemite doubled for that park in the footage that was filmed for this sequence. This was basically a gag sequence, where the two officers get lost and suddenly find themselves at the base of the famous sculpture of the four presidents—only to reveal to the audience that a fifth, female president had been added to the monument sometime in the intervening centuries. The problem was, preview audiences didn't seem to find this even remotely amusing, and thus the sequence, one of two done by Syd Dutton and Bill Taylor of Illusion Arts, was dropped from the film. Another shot cut was a special effects sunrise whipped up to cover for unobliging weather and intruding smoke from forest fires.

Still another "lost" effect involved a Twentieth-Century space probe model built by Greg Jein, based on pictures of NASA's Pioneer 5. This model, six feet long, was constructed around a real satellite dish, but it was non-functioning, so that Robert Lyons of Associates and Ferren had to rework it and install a motor so that it could spin on its mount. The basic plan was to have the Klingon ship piloted by Captain Klaa—the redoubtable Bird of Prey model— encounter the old Earth probe and blast it to pieces using it for target practice. After a number of pyrotechnic and lighting effects were tried, Ferren's effects team was quite pleased with their work on this scene, but the sequence was dropped for reasons never clearly explained.

For the final campfire scene, and the return to Yosemite National Park, Paramount built a forest set and employed Illusion Arts to create a matte shot to show the grandeur of the park under the stars. Shatner, who was still reeling from his exposure to the Hudson Valley School exhibit, decided to go for a full-on Albert Bierstadt effect: Pulling back from the live-action of himself, Leonard Nimoy and DeForest Kelley indulging in an old-fashioned campfire get-together, the camera would pull slowly back until their campfire was just a tiny spark seen from miles above. (This was inspired also by Shatner's viewing of the short film "Powers of Ten," which zooms up from a couple picnicking in a park to a view of the Earth from outer space.)

Bill Taylor of Illusion Arts recalled what a staggering effort this would have been if it had been filmed in accordance with Shatner's directorial desires; it would have required a number of large matte paintings, and would have necessitated flawless dissolves form one matte painting to the next. Things were drastically toned down as the sequence was finally filmed. The forest set, with campfire, was filmed from high up in the rafters of the Paramount sound stage, in a wide screen process, with pine branches in front of the camera to suggest that this was a view from higher up in the forest. This footage became a rear projection matted into the large, single matte painting which was ultimately produced. This was then combined with a large star field for the final shot, which also involved simple live animation effects for the river running through the Yosemite Valley. The combined matte and star field measured in at an impressive four by sixteen feet.

ON SCHEDULE

In the rush of the final post-production work, Associates and Ferren were obliged to farm out some of the last-minute effects needed; they were busy reshooting both the exterior shots of the shuttlecraft crash and the rockburst sequence, which Paramount felt had been filmed at the wrong camera speed. Pacific Title augmented some of the bluescreen work done by The Optical House, while Visual Concept Engineering's Peter Kuran completed the final phaser and Transporter effects.

STAR TREK V: THE FINAL FRONTIER was completed and released on schedule. Unfortunately, it was not entirely certain that all this effort had been worthwhile. The film was critically panned— largely regarded as a true bomb of a movie— and attendance was the lowest of any STAR TREK film before or since. Admittedly, home video sales would eventually take the sting out of this for the studio, but for the effects technicians involved—Bran Ferren and all the others—all that was left was the memory of an intense struggle against an impossible deadline.

If nothing else, the people who did the effects for STAR TREK V deserve credit for their dedication under extremely difficult circumstances. They should not be blamed for Shatner's failure as a director by any means. Perhaps the film's flaws were a good thing; Paramount had, at some stages, made various noises about STAR TREK V being the final film in the series. However, it became apparent to all that Gene Roddenberry's vision deserved a much better send-off than could be provided by THE FINAL FRONTIER.

SPECIAL EFFECTS PHOTO GALLERY

The new Klingon ship from STAR TREK: THE MOTION PICTURE. Following the design of the old Klingon ship, this version is very similar but features a great deal more surface detail due to the demands of the big screen.

Overhead view of the Reliant, a view not actually seen in STAR TREK II: THE WRATH OF KHAN.

PHOTO GALLERY

Side view of the Reliant from STAR TREK II: THE WRATH OF KHAN.

From **STAR TREK III: THE SEARCH FOR SPOCK.** The Enterprise returns to the starbase orbiting Earth.

PHOTO GALLERY

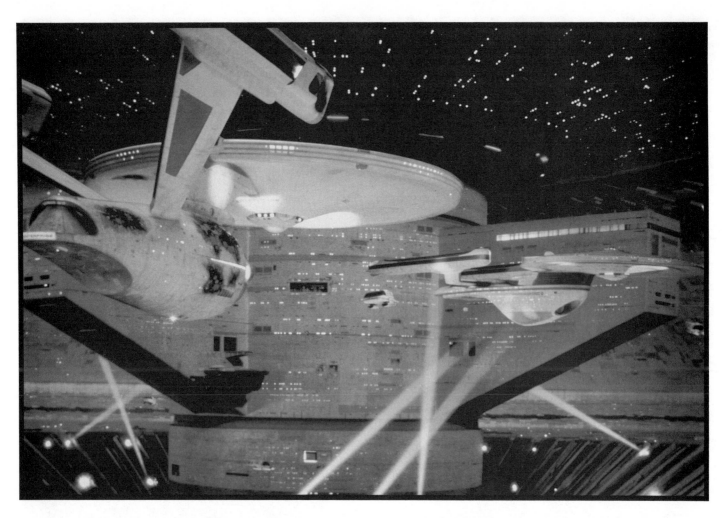

Inside the starbase . . . the scortched Enterprise, the new starship Excelsior (which only appeared in this film, STAR TREK III: THE SEARCH FOR SPOCK), and a small shuttle flying between the two.

PHOTO GALLERY

PHOTO GALLERY

Another new Enterprise, this one from introduced at the conclusion of STAR TREK IV: THE VOYAGE HOME.

PHOTO GALLERY

OPPOSITE: Behind-the-scenes on STAR TREK IV: THE VOYAGE HOME. The
Klingon ship model for the scene in which it crashes into San Francisco Bay.

The final version of the Klingon ship model as it appears on screen when it passes
beneath the Golden Gate Bridge.

In STAR TREK VI: THE UNDISCOVERED COUNTRY, the Enterprise enters warp, the complicated streaking effect originated in STAR TREK: THE MOTION PICTURE.

PHOTO GALLERY

PHOTO GALLERY

The newest Enterprise as seen in STAR TREK: THE NEXT GENERATION.

The Undiscovered Country

After the debacle of the previous installment of the TREK saga, with its weak special effects (admittedly more the result of studio-imposed restrictions than the fault of the hard-working effects team), Paramount Studios was understandably cautious their next time out. STAR TREK V had already managed to be William Shatner's swan song as a director as far as Paramount was concerned. Paramount Studios displayed some wisdom and decided to go with proven talent this time around. They hoped that Leonard Nimoy would direct for a third installment. Although Nimoy would be closely involved with various aspects of the film as producer, he declined to direct. Eventually, Nicholas Meyer, after having written the screenplay from the germ of an idea by Nimoy, would return to direct his second STAR TREK film.

Paramount secured a solid, well-crafted script, a true professional at the helm and the services of; Industrial Light and Magic, Cinema Research (for optical work), Visual Concept Engineering (animation for phasers and Transporters), and Pacific Data Images (crucial wire removals in zero-gravity sequences). Their next concern was to keep both eyes fixed firmly on the budget. The first thing Industrial Light and Magic was faced with was Paramount's insistence that they work only with existing models; absolutely no new sets or ships were to be designed and built for this film!

Money on sets would be saved by re-dressing sets currently in use by STAR TREK: THE NEXT GENERATION. Paramount also packed up all the old space ship models, many over ten years old, and delivered them over to Industrial Light and Magic, who were faced with the daunting task of refitting, and, in many cases, extensively repairing the various models. The internal electrical wiring on many of the ships for example had deteriorated while in storage and needed to be completely redone before any of the models were usable.

The Enterprise utilized by Trumbull in STAR TREK: THE MOTION PICTURE the oldest model to see renewed action in THE UNDISCOVERED COUNTRY. A few cracks in the surface needed to be repaired and concealed, but all in all, the model had survived its long storage pretty well. Of course, it needed to be painted and re-detailed in order to match the new 'A' designation of the second Starship Enterprise.

The old space dock model was still on hand, but only the external model survived; the interior had been misplaced or destroyed, leaving the effects team to rebuild an interior. Budgetary considerations limited this to the single section of the interior that would be seen by the Enterprise as it neared the door leading out from the dock back into the familiar depths of space. For the rendezvous scene, the effects team built the single new model constructed for STAR TREK VI, a new shuttlecraft, and shot the shuttlecraft's approach to the space dock from below. This approach had never been used before despite the obvious logic behind it. It gave a new angle on the same old space dock model and created the much-needed illusion of something new out of something old.

A NEW LOOK

For the Klingon ship, Kronos, Industrial Light and Magic resurrected the Klingon battle cruiser from the opening sequences of ST:TMP. The team found that the deep green model was painted over with a thick layer of white paint. Mark Moore and Bill George decided to work up a new look for the old model and adapted the medieval practice of adding new designs to armor after a significant victory.

They used the old Bird of Prey as General Chang's cloaked Klingon Bird of Prey. In STAR TREK IV: THE VOYAGE HOME, Kirk and crew had used the borrowed Klingon vessel to re-create their old solar slingshot time-travel technique, and the model had been "singed" using black rubber cement to suggest the immense heat endured in the course of that passage. Unfortunately, when the model was unpacked for use in STAR TREK VI, the effects team found that the rubber had hardened onto the model, and the model had to be extensively cleaned up and thoroughly repainted before it could effectively portray the treacherous Chang's deadly, invisible vessel.

The sequence featuring the assassination of Chancellor Gorkon was the work of many hands using various techniques. It stands as one of the most visually striking sequences in the completed film. Supervision of the live action elements of this sequence was the responsibility of second unit director Steve Jaffe. He in turn relied heavily on his producer, Ralph Winter, who had considerable experience shooting zero gravity sequences in STAR TREK V.

Winter came up with the simple yet effective expedient of hiding the wires by tipping the set used in any such sequence; this pretty much made it unnecessary to digitally remove the wires from the shot in all but a few cases. Budget restrictions kept the effects team from using any bluescreen techniques in the sequence, which actually resulted in a better shoot, as blue screen would not have lent itself to the integrated lighting which made this sequence so seamless. One element, a lantern careening about, flashing its light about wildly, could only have been done effectively live on the set— as, in fact, it was.

The purplish Klingon blood floating around in zero gravity was accomplished through the use of computer animation. Liza Keith and Scott Anderson tested out the basic effect, which was then realized by the team of Alex Seiden and Joe Pasquale in the first blood effects shot (the assassin's attack on their first Klingon victim, the Kronos I's Transporter technician). The basic program placed spheres in space, and provided the spheres with a certain amount of "attraction" to each other. As the assassination sequence progresses, different effects personnel came into play. When the first Klingon shot runs into the wall, propelled by the phaser blast, his streaming blood was animated by Jim Mitchell.

WILD IMAGES

Computer technology also was used to create the reflections of the sets seen on the floating globules of blood. This was done by photographing the sets and then applying that visual information with a computer onto the spherical shapes of the blood. Another element of depth was added by having the blood cast shadows on the killers as it drifted by them on their way to the Transporter.

This was largely done by Joe Pasquale who created images which corresponded to the actor's bodies. These images were then animated to correspond with the live-action movements. Finally, they applied "shadows" to these forms using the precise angles and lighting of the live shoot. These shadows were composited along with the other elements, including floating blood in varying degrees of focus depending on its location in the picture, to create an eerily impressive scene of zero-gravity mayhem. Add to this the effect of the tumbling light source shining on the blood and you get an idea of the incredible amount of effort and work that went into this key sequence.

Other elements in this sequence were added by ILM. Pyrotechnic effects were used to make the Klingon uniforms hit by phaser fire tear and burn. Because of the budget, Paramount didn't want to damage too many costumes. These effects were added with computer graphics, including the tear in David Warner's costume when Gorkon is fatally shot.

Various Klingon props were created and built by the maven of modelmakers, Greg Jein. Chancellor Gorkin's cane was one of these creations. Presuming than it was crafted from the bone of some large creature that Gorkon had killed at some point during his life, Jein designed it accordingly; the grip looked like some sort of hip bone, while the length of the cane itself suggested that it was a huge fang. Two canes were built to function as actual canes for David Warner, and two light-weight replicas were crafted for use in the zero-gravity sequence. Other Jein creations floating about in the aftermath of the assassination included a Klingon clipboard, a Klingon goblet, and a number of Klingon laptop computers, which Jein made using the lower half of one of the flying saucers he had created for BATTERIES NOT INCLUDED.

In an interesting side note, designer Nilo Rodis incorporated a reference to another classic television program into the assassination sequence. The assassins wear Federation space suits, presumably for doing outside work on ships in space; the reflecting faceplate was actually made out of protective eye wear. Rodis' tribute came in the form of the serial numbers on the two assassins' helmets. The numbers, E1 02 and E1 11, ostensibly meant Engineering Section One, followed by the crew members number. . . but E1 02 and E1 11 were also the code numbers for a pair of secret agents who made a splash in the 'sixties, Napoleon Solo and Ilya Kuryakin, as portrayed by Robert Vaughn and David McCallum on THE MAN FROM UNCLE.

SONY AND STAR TREK

When Captain Kirk and "Bones" McCoy beam over to the Kronos to help Gorkon, DeForest Kelley used a number of futuristic medical tools which were designed by Greg Jein. One item used in this scene employed twentieth century technology to represent that of the twenty-fourth: rather than build a Klingon medical monitor from scratch, Jein went to a local video equipment store and purchased a Sony eight-millimeter video monitor, which was dressed up to look like a Klingon artifact. The Klingon innards displayed on this screen were actually a pre-recorded tape that was played live on the monitor as the scene of Gorkon's death was being filmed.

For the arrest of Kirk and McCoy, it was deemed necessary to have the Klingons draw their phasers. This proved to be a problem. The phaser holsters worn by the Klingons were survivors of STAR TREK: THE MOTION PICTURE. The phasers inside them were the redesigned Klingon phasers left over from STAR TREK II: THE WRATH OF KHAN. The only way that these phasers ever fit into their mismatched holsters was when the muzzles were cut off of them.

This explains why the Klingons in STAR TREK III did their dirty work with fists and knives: they didn't really have any complete phasers on them! Greg Jein came to the rescue here and designed new muzzles for the phasers so that they could be holstered and drawn as needed, in full view of the camera.

Of course, Kirk and McCoy are soon whisked away to the Klingon home world, where they are charged with the murder of Chancellor Gorkon. Here, Klingon guards wielded vicious tridents with illuminated points and blade-like handgrips; these were more creations of Greg Jein. Jein also devised the gavel glove worn by the albino judge in this sequence, which consisted of a cracked steel ball held in the grip of the metallic glove.

When it was discovered that the actor playing the judge had arthritis, Jein hollowed out more of the inside of the glove in order to provide it with more padding. Originally, light was intended to emit from the cracks in the ball whenever the judge slammed his gavel-glove down, but the actor, arthritis or not, got carried away and the light inside the prop broke after only a few impacts.

A LUCKY BREAK

The Klingon courtroom sequence was originally planned to be filmed in a large sound stage but was bumped to a smaller set. Herman Zimmerman, production designer for STAR TREK VI (and a veteran of the first two seasons of STAR TREK: THE NEXT GENERATION) saw this as a fortuitous change, as sixty-five extras were all that were available to represent the approximately three thousand Klingons who gather to witness the condemnation of Kirk.

Although only three rows of Klingons were shown, the illusion was created that there were more and more in the higher levels of the court; a matte painting added to the set added to this effect. Michael Dorn also had a hand in portraying the Klingons up in the highest reaches of the courtroom, as seen in the first establishing shot of the scene: a miniature set was built to be composited with the live action later, and populated with two hundred Worf dolls bought at nearby toy stores! These 1/72 scale Worfs were made to move back and forth angrily through the use of cams attached to motors run by the motion control system. Small Christmas lights were used to suggest the angry Klingons' lighted spears.

The miniature set was actually filmed on its side, in a smoke-filled room in order to get that murky Klingon atmosphere. Live action Klingons were also filmed for the uppermost of "live" tiers in the courtroom, in order to be composited with the miniature higher levels and its two hundred plastic Worfs.

Makeup for STAR TREK VI was another area of the budget seriously curtailed by Paramount's austerity measures. The makeup team, under the supervision of Michael Mills (who was appointed to the position by his predecessor, Marvin Westmore, when he bowed out of STAR TREK VI), managed to create an incredible number of makeups for the shoot. Ken Myers would be serving as Michael Mills' number two man, a direct reversal of the relationship they had had on STAR TREK V. (Both men had also worked together on BACK TO THE FUTURE II and III, so they were used to chaotic work situations.)

In charge of the makeups for Vulcans, Romulans and, most crucially, Klingons, was Richard Snell, while the experienced Edward French handled the bulk of the other multifarious alien creatures encountered in the film. In fact, despite its budgetary limitations, THE UN-DISCOVERED COUNTRY would prove to have more alien makeups than any other TREK film . In addition to over twenty primary characters who needed specialized makeups, prosthetic makeups often were needed for over one hundred secondary characters— on a daily basis!

OLD IS GOOD

For the aliens who had actually appeared on the original STAR TREK television series, it was decided to go back to the original Fred Phillips makeup concepts. Especially in the case of Spock. Leonard Nimoy insisted on having his final performance as Spock look as close to the original classic television version (but not all the way back to the look of Spock in the first STAR TREK pilot, of course). Edward French reworked some of these for modern tastes, but the basic designs were pretty much the same, avoiding the forehead prosthesis used for Romulans on THE NEXT GENERATION, for instance, in favor of the less complex design used back in the sixties. French also did much of the actual work on his own re-workings of those classic designs.

For Nimoy's Spock makeup, more than the right shape (the original ears had been longer and more forward-oriented than in the other film versions) was needed; Nimoy wanted the precise yellowish skin tone of Spock from the series. To achieve this, Michael Mills had to find sixties-vintage manufactured Max Factor makeup, and from this he recreated the exact tone .

For Mark Lenard's appearance as Sarek, Michael Mills called upon his friend Jerry Quist, the number two makeup man for STAR TREK: THE NEXT GENERATION. Quist devised a makeup for Sarek that reflected both his younger appearance and his more aged one. No such problems were presented in the case of Lieutenant Valeris. Kim Catrall had come into the project with her own design for her character's makeup and hairstyle. Her skin color was designed to be much less sallow than that of Spock.

Most of the appliances for Klingon makeup were designed by Richard Snell, with input from Nilo Rodis and Nicholas Meyer. Further complicating issues was the renowned Shakespearaean actor Christopher Plummer, who wanted to stand out from the Klingon herd. Thus, the Klingon bone ridge was played down. Instead, at Nicholas Meyer's insistence that Chang resemble the late Israeli leader Moshe Dayan, Chang soon sported an eyepatch. The concept of the patch being literally bolted to the orbits of Chang's skull was derived form one of Nilo Rodis' designs. Plummer's input included the notion that one of the bolts be loosened (suggesting a loose screw!). He also declined to use the wig designed for him, which obliged Richard Snell to redesign the back of Chang's head to some extent.

PUTTING ON THE MAKEUP

David Warner's Gorkon makeup was suggested by Nicholas Meyer's choice of historic figures to represent the audience's uncertainty about the character: Abraham Lincoln and Captain Ahab. This makeup was designed by Margaret Bessera.

For the Klingon courtroom sequence, the makeup team had to turn out quite a few makeup jobs: eighteen speaking Klingon characters (including Michael Dorn as the ancestor of Worf), another thirty full makeups worthy of close camera scrutiny, forty latex masks that required make-up application for midrange shots and, for the distant background, fifty or more plastic Klingon masks.

Once Kirk and McCoy get to Rura Penthe, the dreaded ice-swept penal colony planet, they encounter the shapeshifing Martia, portrayed by Iman. To avoid covering up Iman's unique features, it was decided to avoid any heavy effects makeup for her character. But to create an alien look for her, it was decided to give her an avian appearance. Ed French, in close conjunction with hairstylist Jan Alexander, came up with a wig made entirely of feathers. The bird theme went farther than that: every bit of hair seen on Iman, even her eyebrows, were made of small feathers. Her eyes, yellow and spotted, were special contact lenses created by Richard Snell, who also created the special contact lenses worn by Marina Sirtis and Brent Spiner on STAR TREK: THE NEXT GENERATION.

The establishing shot of Rura Penthe was created by Matte World. For the distant live action figures composited into this matte painting, Brook Benton filmed extras walking on sheets of white plastic on a San Francisco beach on an overcast day. This footage of people walking against a white background was rear-projected onto the matte rather than being composited optically; Paramount was still keeping bluescreen work to the barest minimum.

For the alien who picks a fight with Captain Kirk, Ed French came up with an appropriately craggy makeup design. French also used fluorescent makeup so that ultraviolet light could be used to trigger changes in the creature's coloration. He utilized the assistance of a company called Wildfire, who had worked on BILL AND TED'S BOGUS JOURNEY and ALIEN 3; they also created Geordi's transformation in STAR TREK: THE NEXT GENERATION's fourth season episode "Identity Crisis." The ultraviolet-sensitive paints produced by Wildfire are transparent, so the different shades can be layered for a variety of UV-triggered effects. The company also provided the use of special lighting equipment they have created, which can illuminate their paints from as far away as sixty feet.

NEVER TRUST AN ALIEN

To explain how the aging Kirk can defeat this lumbering creature (besides the fortuitous kick in the knees, that is) French had one of his assistants squash the horns on the creature's makeup, suggesting that this was a bully who lost a lot of fights but never seemed to get the picture. Nicholas Meyer came up with the further idea of cranking up the intensity of the ultraviolet light once Kirk wins the fight, thus giving the distinct impression that the alien is throbbing with pain.

Eventually, Martia apparently helps Kirk and McCoy escape; it's really a deadly set-up. This is where morphing comes into play: first, Martia transforms into the Brute, an Ed French makeup design worn by Tom Morga. The Brute makeup consisted of five prosthetics: the forehead, the cheeks (with ears attached), the upper nose with mouth, and the lower jaw. Morga also wore upper and lower dentures, the upper ones being more pronounced to create the proper brutish look. Dodie French constructed the Brute's body suit, while French designed the hands and feet of the creature.

After the Brute's strength gets Kirk and McCoy so far, the creature morphs again, this time into a little girl. For the morphing, the live action footage shot on the set served as the basic working material. This live action footage was then scanned into the computer and the actors' images blended. The Brute's transformation into the girl marked the very first time that morphing had been utilized with a character in motion. Further complicating this sequence was the extreme disparity in size between the Brute and the girl.

Soon afterwards, Martia becomes herself again, but it is discovered that she is in on a plot to murder Kirk and McCoy. In the ensuing fight, Iman morphs into William Shatner. Here, Martia becomes Kirk while she is talking with him. This entailed filming both actors speaking identical lines; this still was not a perfect solution, because the shape of Iman's and Shatner's mouths were extremely different even when forming the same sounds. But ILM's computer graphics wizard John Berton, in charge of computer animation, pulled off the morphing sequences flawlessly.

Spock and the Enterprise arrive just in time to beam Kirk and McCoy to safety. Chekhov uses a Greg Jein designed device, a lighter-sized welding torch, to get the manacles off of the two liberated prisoners. Spock must then discover the location of the next assassination attempt, and learns that it is on the planet Khitomer, where a crucial peace conference is underway. But first, the Enterprise, aided by the Sulu-captained Excelsior, must get past General Chang's deadly, invisible Bird of Prey.

IT'S NEVER EASY

Motion control for the battle sequence was handled by Peter Daulton. The motion control on the establishing shot of the sequence, which sweeps by the Enterprise from the Bird of Prey's viewpoint, involved such radical movement that it was necessary to move the bluescreen behind the Enterprise model in order to keep it in place. The bluescreen had to be moved a hundred and eighty degrees for this shot. This difficult shot was cut and only about one third of it actually made it into the final cut of STAR TREK VI. As with so many science fiction films, STAR TREK VI had its share of effects that were either cut from the film, or scrapped before they could even be realized.

Originally, the principal characters were to be introduced in a number of scenes which were never filmed. Scotty, for example, was to have been first seen giving a lecture in a hangar while the Klingon Bird of Prey, apparently raised from the bottom of San Francisco Bay, was being examined. Kirk was to have been first encountered as he got into a flying taxicab. Another shot that was dropped from later in the film would have had Spock, en route to rescue Kirk and McCoy, slide the Enterprise into an asteroid belt and drift on through using the asteroids as cover.)

For the all-important photon torpedoes used in the battle sequence, ILM's Bill George decided to go for a less "pretty" looking effect and came up with a torpedo effect that looked a good deal more deadly. The motion control on the torpedoes also suggested, for once, that these were "smart" missiles which sought their prey. And one of the Bird of Prey's photon torpedoes goes right through a section of the Enterprise, an effect that Bill George had always dreamed of doing. A replacement section of the dish was built and the effect, filmed upside down for the proper zero-gravity look, was filmed to dramatic effect.

Just in the nick of time, Spock figures out how to locate the cloaked ship by tracking its exhaust gases. With time a premium, Spock and McCoy must specially alter a photon torpedo to track the exhaust; in the cramped space of the torpedo bay, McCoy uses surgical instruments—created and built by Scott Snyder of Greg Jein's model shop. These instruments had lights inside them so that DeForest Kelley and Leonard Nimoy could trigger the electronics themselves. The altered torpedo hits the Bird of Prey, destroying the cloaking effect, and leaving it open to a one-two torpedo punch from the Excelsior, which has arrived on the scene, and the Enterprise. (The gusto with which Shatner gives the order to fire the fatal torpedo should qualify as a special effect in its own right.)

SLIGHT ALTERATIONS

The destruction of the Bird of Prey originally done with pyrotechnic elements placed in the frame with the ship by use of motion control. The final explosion was the actual destruction of a model ship made from a cast of one of the Bird of Prey models used in the crash sequence at the end of STAR TREK IV: THE VOYAGE HOME. But the original model had its wings back for landing, so the new model derived from it had to be altered so that its wings would be in combat position. Once this was attended to, three models were made, cast of brittle epoxy, with various model parts and pieces of metal and other material inside to represent interior parts of the Bird of Prey thrown out by the explosion. The footage of the exploding model, filmed against a black background, then replaced the motion control model by use of a simple lap dissolve.

For the interior view of the death of Chang, Steve Jaffe and Ron Roose rigged up a dummy Chang in the same position as the last shot of Christopher Plummer, and then exploded it. Then they culled a mere three frames of this and matched it with the Plummer footage in order to create the subliminal impression that Chang had really gone down (or up, in this instance) with the ship.

With this impediment out of the way, the Enterprise and the Excelsior can proceed to Khitomer. The establishing shot of Khitomer was a matte painting (executed by Michael Pangrazio of Matte World) combined with two live-action elements. The first was footage of a community center in Brandeis, California, a circular building, with extras carrying the flags of all planets in front of it. The second live element, filmed at the Fireman's Fund building in Novato, California, featured a Klingon and a Starfleet officer on a balcony, with a man-made lake reflecting light in the background. Pangrazio's painting linked the two live action elements while extending the balcony and adding futuristic details to the buildings.

For the many aliens in attendance at the Khitomer peace conference, Ed French came up with a number of makeups. (As noted, the look of the Romulans here was more in line with the classic TREK look than it was with the makeup later established for THE NEXT GENERATION.) French even came up with the swinish Tellurites, last seen in "Journey To Babel." His references to the past went beyond the obvious STAR TREK material: many of the aliens on Khitomer were based on the design of various creatures designed by makeup artist Wah Chang for THE OUTER LIMITS.

The Klingon assassin foiled by Scotty in this sequence carries a modular assault rifle in a case, somewhat reminiscent of Lawrence Harvey in THE MANCHURIAN CANDIDATE. This rifle was designed by Greg Jein, basing parts of it on casts made from a real assault rifle but sculptured to give it the appropriate Klingon look, which Jein surmises evolved from their origin in the seas of their planet (different designers have different theories about Klingons, but what the heck).

SETTING THE SCORE EVEN

With the plot to destroy peace foiled, the Enterprise's Captain and Chief Medical Officer are cleared, and a new era of near-harmony between the Federation and the Klingon Empire dawns, with the Romulans snarling under their breaths on the sidelines. The Enterprise crew is decommissioned but Kirk decides to take her out for one more spin, and the actors sign off.

THE UNDISCOVERED COUNTY set things back on an even keel after the imbalance created by STAR TREK V: THE FINAL FRONTIER, and provided a look forward to THE NEXT GENERATION as well. Industrial Light and Magic proved that it was possible to create superb special effects within the limitations of schedule and budget set by Paramount Studios; the four TREK films graced by their work stand head and shoulders above the two which had their effects created by others, perhaps a coincidence in terms of plot and direction, but a fact nevertheless. Industrial Light and Magic, by this point, had already helped launch STAR TREK: THE NEXT GENERATION—but beyond their initial contribution, the effects for that show would themselves be created by a new generation of special effects artists.

After being given a brief send-off by Industrial Light & Magic, this series has gone on to present some of the best and most intriguing special effects ever seen on the small screen.

8

The Next Generation
Television Again, With Budget

When STAR TREK—THE NEXT GENERATION premiered in 1987, much was made of its tie-in to Lucasfilm's Industrial Light and Magic. However, because ILM was geared towards motion picture schedules and not TV, Their involvement was limited.

Like STAR TREK: THE MOTION PICTURE, the first NEXT GENERATION episode, "Encounter At Farpoint," was slow moving and all too enamored of its own special effects. The special effects for this and the second episode was provided by Industrial Light & Magic. Unfortunately, ILM was too expensive and other effects teams were sought out.

Also crucially involved in the general effects look of THE NEXT GENERATION were the designers of the show. Andrew Probert served as Senior Consulting Illustrator for the series, while Mike Okuda was the primary scenic artist. Rick Sternbach also contributed a great deal to the series design in collaboration with these others.

Andrew Probert first worked with the STAR TREK universe when he designed a good number of the spaceships seen in STAR TREK: THE MOTION PICTURE. He also did a lot of television work prior to joining the NEXT GENERATION team. AIRWOLF, STREETHAWK, and BATTLESTAR GALACTICA all number among his past accomplishments, as does the motion picture INDIANA JONES AND THE TEMPLE OF DOOM. Probert began his move to professional work when he was inspired by Ralph McQuarrie's work on STAR WARS. Probert arranged to meet McQuarrie through the pretext of an interview for his college newspaper. Afterwards, McQuarrie recommended Probert for the project that ultimately became BATTLESTAR GALACTICA.

Probert was responsible for the final design of the Cylons. For STAR TREK: THE MOTION PICTURE, Probert contributed significant design work on the space drydock, the Vulcan shuttle, and various other spacecraft, up to and including the final design for the Enterprise itself. That design featured a separation line between the saucer and body of the Enterprise, since one of the design ideas kicking around at the time was the notion of the saucer separating from the rest of the vessel. This was not realized in the movie, but Probert was on hand when it finally was on STAR TREK: THE NEXT GENERATION.

Probert's first official job for THE NEXT GENERATION was to design the new bridge for the latest D-class model Enterprise. Paramount's original plan was to create a bridge four times larger than that ultimately settled on. The conference room is a separate set; the bridge itself is actually a little bit smaller than the bridge set for the STAR TREK movies, except for the fact that it has a higher ceiling. Probert also had to incorporate the notion, provided by Gene Roddenberry, that technology would have advanced significantly enough to allow crew members to sit comfortably at their work stations instead of hunching over them.

Probert's original design also included the main transporter facility being just off the bridge. Roddenberry squelched this idea for dramatic reasons, feeling that the turbolift would be a good place for the characters to indulge in a bit of expository dialogue on their way to the transporter room. Another idea of Probert's was to place Captain Picard's office on an upper level so that when he came out of his office he could look down on the bridge. This was ultimately scrapped as well, perhaps to de-emphasize the military aspects of the situation.

One idea of Probert's did make it into the bridge set for THE NEXT GENERATION. Something no other Enterprise had on its bridge, or perhaps even anywhere else on board the ship, for that matter. . . a bathroom. In an alcove near the entrance to the conference room there is a door labelled "head." (That term for bathroom has a nautical origin deriving from the general location of such facilities on board ships.) Unfortunately, Probert's extension of this concept entailing stencilled silhouettes of various life forms on the door and colored lines leading to the appropriate facility for each species, was never carried out. To this date, no one has actually seen the interior of a twenty-fourth century bathroom. (Presumably, there being only *one* on the bridge, the facilities are unisex, Phyllis Schaffly's greatest nightmare realized.)

Probert consciously echoed the design of the original television show's Enterprise in a number of ways. The schematics of the Enterprise on the wall of the bridge are located exactly where they were on the original set, off to one side of the turbolift. Probert also added a red flashing light at the bottom of the viewscreen which comes on during alerts, much as the light between Sulu and Chekov on the original show signalled red alerts.

Probert also came up with the idea of a separate battle bridge for use in case of saucer separations. In fact, Probert was they key figure in the design of the NCC-1701-D. One idea never realized was that instead of a battle bridge, there would actually be a smaller battleship which separated from the saucer. But there is one Probert design that is part of the Enterprise as it now exists, even though it has never been used in the series: on the underside of the saucer section is a small, flying-saucer like attachment. This may look like merely another part of the overall design, but it is actually the Captain's Yacht, a thirty-five person craft which Probert imagined would be used in super-crucial diplomatic missions. (In the Enterprise model kit made by the Ertl company, this craft is actually detachable.)

THE FERENGI SHIP

Probert also designed the look of the Ferengi spacecraft. Although the Ferengi (whose name is actually the Persian word from which the English word "foreigner" is derived) have devolved into comical characters, they were originally intended as the new villains for the series and Probert made their ship look menacing. The actual appearance of the Ferengi went through an astounding number of varied permutations before it reached its present form. This was also the result of Probert's endeavors. He strived to visualize, Gene Roddenberry's concept of that most alien of races.

It was also Probert's idea that Picard would have a model of his previous command, the Stargazer, in his ready room. He took it upon himself to build one, utilizing a standard (old version) Enterprise model kit and adapting it. To Probert's bemusement, the producers of THE NEXT GENERATION, although they allowed the model to stay on the set, declined to regard it as being representative of the Stargazer—but when the episode "The Battle" was about to be filmed, it was Probert's model which served as the basis of the four-foot effects model which was built to portray the Stargazer in that episode!

Another veteran of STAR TREK: THE MOTION PICTURE was renowned illustrator Rick Sternbach. Sternbach was also inspired to get into his field by the work of Ralph McQuarrie. Sternbach's reputation was solidly entrenched as the result of his work on the popular Carl Sagan science program COSMOS. Sternbach also worked on Disney's THE BLACK HOLE, John Carpenter's HALLOWEEN II, and the television series THE GREATEST AMERICAN HERO.

In an interesting side note, Rick Sternbach also painted the picture of the Enterprise that hangs in Captain Picard's ready room; this is the original painting, which was reproduced for a cereal giveaway promotion by Cheerios a few years back.

Hailing from Hawaii, scenic artist Mike Okuda works on all the graphics utilized in the series. Okuda had some background in commercials and sent some samples to Paramount when he heard that STAR TREK IV: THE VOYAGE HOME was going into production. Okuda had always been a big fan of STAR TREK and was extremely motivated to get involved with it. His persistence paid off, and his ensuing work on STAR TREK IV led to his position on the fledgling new series.

MULTI DIMENSIONAL

Not only does Okuda create all the read-outs seen on the show, all the signs and control panels, he even adds to the set. Some of the doors seen in the hallway sets are simply graphic applications with no actual door. Alien lettering and symbols is also his department, in which he is assisted by graphics artist Cari Thomas, who worked on MAX HEADROOM. Mike Okuda created one vital element of THE NEXT GENERATION when he solved the design problem that had been keeping Andrew Probert up nights. . . Geordi's visor. Okuda brought in the plastic barrette which became the basis for the visor; all Probert had to do was enlarge it and alter the design so that it could be worn over a human's face.

In the Peabody-award winning first season episode "The Big Goodbye," Okuda and his colleagues created all the texts that Data scans on his computer console while researching the character of Dixon Hill. Even though the texts flashed by too fast for the television audience to read them, they had to have the overall design appearance of old pulp detective magazines from the nineteen-thirties and forties. Okuda assembled dummy texts for this purpose. To cover the fact that the titles of these imaginary texts *were* frequently legible, even if only on a subliminal level, Okuda and his team gave the pieces titles as well as an author's name in the byline: that of Tracy Torme, who scripted that particular episode.

For the special eye effects for Deanna Troi and Lieutenant Data, THE NEXT GENERATION turned to Richard Snell, who had created special contact lenses for various STAR TREK features and would do so again in the future; the dark contacts worn by Marina Sirtis and the yellow ones worn by Brent Spiner were Snell's custom creations. (Astute observers will note that Data's eyes were a more pronounced shade of yellow during the early seasons.)

Industrial Light and Magic produced some fifty special effects shots for "Encounter At Farpoint," but a new team of specialists were hired by the time the second episode was in production. In fact, two teams have worked on the series producing its special effects since 1987. One team consists of Robert Legato and coordinator Gary Hutzel while they alternate with another team comprised of Dan Curry and Ron Moore. They began with a weekly special effects budget of seventy-five thousand dollars, only twenty-five thousand dollars more per week than the old STAR TREK had for its effects shots twenty years before. However, the modern technology surrounding both videotape and motion control gave them the advantages of speed which the old series didn't have.

A ROUGH ROAD

The road to video was not a smooth one. In fact, associate producer Peter Lauritson had a difficult time convincing Paramount to go with video special effects. Paramount leaned heavily towards film. This would enable them to take THE NEXT GENERATION pilot and re-edit it as a film for European release and other international markets. An international video release would have been complicated by the different video formats used in different parts of the world.

Lauritson sold them on the video approach by demonstrating that the video effects budget would be much lower than film. This, for Paramount, offset any monies that might be lost, and also seemed to make the series a more viable proposition in the long run. And since THE NEXT GENERATION's special effects are shot on film and then transferred to videotape for both editing and composition purposes, the result is a sharper resolution to the image which is why the new Enterprise never looks grainy or fuzzy the way the old TV Enterprise often did. While the special effects on the sixties series are still often impressive even twenty-five years later (particularly if you've seen one of the old shows projected on a large screen), the new generation of effects has opened the show up to more possibilities.

Of course, STAR TREK: THE NEXT GENERATION is actually shot on film, both in the live action sequences and in the special effects shots. Video comes into play in post production, when practically every element is transferred to video and blended together seamlessly.

Due to modern computer animation techniques, a phaser beam can be drawn right on the frame of film when it's being edited on videotape. Other previously used visual effects can be sometimes combined to create something new such as a cloud image or a water pattern which can be used to create an unusual looking force field. Stock footage can be employed, such as using the orbiting space station first seen in THE SEARCH FOR SPOCK wherein the new Enterprise is substituted for the old Enterprise. This has turned up in THE NEXT GENERATION on an average of once a season since 1987.

While THE NEXT GENERATION is filmed at Paramount Studios in Hollywood, the special effects teams originally worked across town in Santa Monica at Digital Magic. There the optical effects were shot on film and then sent out to video transfer lab to be transferred to D-1 digital videotape where the special effects technicians can later combine various effects to create a single image. For instance, the Enterprise is filmed separately from its lights as the use of motion control cameras allows a separate pass to be made of the model with its lights glowing to be superimposed on the previous shot of the Enterprise now on videotape. The engine lights will be a brighter exposure with some diffusion while the cabin lights, filmed on yet another pass, will be dimmer. When composited in one shot, it's impossible to tell that it's multiple shots combined into a single image.

GROWING NUMBERS

Working on videotape allows color correcting and even light balancing to be done which could not be as easily accomplished working with an effect on film. When effects are combined on film in an optical printer, the work goes down a generation in quality each time, thereby resulting in the grainy appearance of some special visual effects seen in past motion pictures.

The special effects technicians brought in after ILM had done their work on the pilot were led to believe that about ten new shots would be needed for each additional episode. This quickly escalated to an average of 60 to a high of 100 new shots per show. Even in the first season the producers were hoping to find stock shots to match the demands of certain scripts. But there were no scenes available which could show the edge of the universe ("Where No One Has Gone Before") or the Enterprise being knocked end over end through space at warp speed ("When The Bough Breaks").

Complicating this was that the new effects teams inherited the Enterprise model built by ILM. It was six feet long and was lacking in the kind of detail necessary for close-ups. At six feet in length, it was too large to do a true long-shot. But since they also had a two foot model available, they were able to make use of that one as well. A four foot model was built for season three which has been used for the new special effects shots of the Enterprise ever since.

When the four foot model was built, Gary Hutzel developed a neon transformer which enabled them to change the lighting scheme on the Enterprise model with the flick of a switch. By contrast each lighting change on the old six foot model took an hour.

THE NEXT GENERATION showed something which had never been seen before. . .the shields. In general use, they are invisible— but the whole point of the shields is to protect the Enterprise against attack, and it was surmised that the shield *would* be visible when under fire, not the whole shield of course, but the section under attack. Dan Curry devised this effect. First he bought some sheets of silver Mylar at a fabric store. With Ron Moore, Curry shot various lighting effects, directing light at the mylar with a mirror and interposing a reflective silver pom-pom and shaking it in order to create moving light. Filming this through various filters and prisms, Curry and Moore came up with a very glowing, prismatic rainbow effect, which was then wraped into a sphere by use of computer imaging. Portions of this sphere were wiped into the image to create the effect of sections of the shield glowing as they were hit by phaser fire or other weaponry.

SAVING MONEY

Not all optical shots are time consuming or expensive. In the first season episode "When The Bough Breaks," Robert Legato's team had to create a shot of the power station seen near the end of the episode. They built models and shot them against a black wall which was heavily backlit and then matted that into a miniature which created an effect of looking at a ledge which appeared to be a hundred feet off the floor. The shot cost only about three thousand dollars to accomplish. Had they farmed it out to another company, the shot would probably have cost at least thirty-five thousand dollars to realize. In this case, ingenuity won out over necessity, and a sizeable lump of cash was saved.

The first effects team to sign on after ILM was the one headed by Robert Legato, later to be known as the A Team. When it became apparent that more effects would be called for per episode than initially anticipated, a B Team was created. To head this unit, NEXT GENERATION producer Peter Lauritson sought and obtained the services of Dan Curry. Before signing on with THE NEXT GENERATION, Dan Curry worked with Cinema Research corporation. There, he was involved in titles work as well as various special effects for such movies as TOP GUN and Stephen Spielberg's INDIANA JONES AND THE TEMPLE OF DOOM. His first effects work for THE NEXT GENERATION would be on the episode "Datalore."

The head of whichever of these two special effects unit is working on an episode invariably supervises the on-set effects filmed during the normal principal photography schedule of seven to eight days. The film editors then spend two weeks assembling the footage and deliver the final cut of the live action part of the show to the special effects team. The special effects teams get the script for a show and plan out their shots.

They are unable to do any real work on it until the live action footage has been shot and edited together. From that they'll know how much time is allotted for the demands of the visual effects and they generally then have from eight to ten days to deliver. The special visual effects involves from five to nine days of shooting the Enterprise and other ships with five or six days to composite all of the elements together into the finished shots. Specific instructions are then given on where to edit each scene into the episode.

"The Battle," in which a Ferengi captain seeks a strange revenge on Captain Picard, was far from being a great episode, but, as directed by Rob Bowman, was one of the first NEXT GENERATION episodes to utilize different camera techniques. In order to emphasize the strangeness of Picard's experience returning to his old vessel the Stargazer, Bowman utilized a Steadicam. The Stargazer itself (Picard's first command) was a model built by Greg Jein's model studio, a three-and-a-half foot model that was Jein's favorite among those he has created for the series.

COMPUTERS SAVE THE DAY

"Datalore" was the obligatory 'evil twin' episode, directed by Bowman. Bowman did a creditable job aided largely by Brent Spiner's good work in the dual role of Data/Lore. This marked the first episode worked on by Dan Curry. For the sequence where Data is opened up in order to learn how to reassemble Lore, footage of Data's interior were matted into the medical monitors, but the footage did not look like anything but a bad matte. To alleviate this, the frame was placed into the Mirage, the same computer effects device used to create the shields. The Mirage was used to create lighting effects which made it appear that lights were reflecting off the glass of the monitor.

Crucial to the success of "Datalore," was the need to create flawless split screen images of the two androids, portrayed by Brent Spiner. Fortunately, motion control and computer technology make it possible to move the split line in the picture to accommodate the movements of the actor portraying both roles. In one scene, Lore offers Data a drink of champagne; the two androids are standing on opposite sides of a table. Lore poured the champagne and set the glass for data down on the table, all the while staying behind the line of the split. Using a soft-edge wipe to obscure the line, technician Fred Raimondi moved the line, allowing Data to pick up the glass without having his hand disappear behind the line. Matching lighting and color between the two takes of Brent Spiner was the only task that remained; the scene appears flawless unless the viewer happens to be staring directly at the glass of champagne, which went flat between takes.

In "The Last Outpost," Robert Legato devised a means of panning in a shot involving a bluesceen effect. Actually, the camera did not pan at all in this scene in which Riker looks out over a ledge to a not-yet-matted-in landscape. Instead, Legato shot the scene in an anamorphic (scope) process, which created a wider-than usual image. This was then panned and scanned. In this case, the scanning created the illusion of a pan executed by the camera. Then, using an identical panning motion, the effects shots (also shot anamorphic) were matched with the bluescreen that Jonathan Frakes had actually been looking at. This was a simple, inexpensive and time-efficient means of creating an effects shot with movement, and stands as one of Robert Legato's greatest innovations.

One of the better first season episodes was "Conspiracy," which went all out with its exploding-head sequence and gratuitous grub-eating. The head sequence, which earned the episode an advisory notice and a large viewer response, was accomplished as follows. First of all, special effects coordinator Dick Brownfield found an old latex cast of a head— actor Paul Newman's, to be precise— stuffed it full of meat, set it up on a dummy and set off an explosive charge, blasting the jury-rigged head to pieces. At the Post Group, a matte was made of the face of the actor portraying the doomed Remick; this was composited over the pyrotechnic dummy footage and wiped away selectively for the phaser burn preceding the actual head explosion, which showed skin boiling away, although the actor's actual teeth and eyes lingered. Pieces of meat kept turning up on the set, as well as on adjacent soundstages, for days after this sequence's original footage was filmed!

Writer Tracy Torme, adapting a story by Robert Sabaroff to THE NEXT GENERATION, had hoped to make "Conspiracy" a commentary on the Iran/Contra Affair, but this potentially controversial notion was nixed. A plot by Starfleet officers out to undermine the Prime Directive (already introduced six episodes before in "Coming of Age"), turns out to be the result of an infestation of alien insects, not part of Torme's original approach. There was just no way he could get away with suggesting that the Federation was anything less than a perfect government. Retained was the dubious ending and the explicit violence, although Torme was not behind the exploding head at the end of the episode, which was put in by the producers.

SECOND SEASON

THE NEXT GENERATION's second season saw the departure of production designer Herman Zimmerman and his replacement by Richard James; Zimmerman jumped ship from one Enterprise to another, and provided design for STAR TREK V: THE FINAL FRONTIER. Richard James was yet another NEXT GENERATION staff member who had previously done production design on BATTLESTAR GALACTICA, a science fiction series that easily set the record for the most obvious recycling of effects shots.

The starfields for the premiere season of THE NEXT GENERATION had been made of black duvetyne with glitter glued on at random. James informed David Livingston and Rick Berman of how starfields had been created on BATTLESTAR GALACTICA: the glitter stars had been glued manually onto black velvet backgrounds. More expensive materials and time consuming hand work didn't appeal to the producers, but they went with the idea, which proved to pay off better in the long run. Richard James remains in his production design capacity to this day.

Sometimes necessity is the mother of invention. In "A Matter of Honor," renegade Klingons attempt to enlist Worf's assistance. Director Rob Bowman solved a pressing props problem when in a fit of inspiration, he 'invented' a Klingon ladder by appropriating a bicycle rack from the studio lot and mounting it sideways!

THIRD SEASON

Sometimes special effects are called upon to highlight the natural, as in the case of "Sarek." When the visiting Ambassador Sarek sheds a tear at a concert, much to the astonishment of Picard, the tear on Mark Lenard's cheek simply did not have the visual feel hoped for. So Dan Curry shot an effect using a drop of milk on a piece if black paper; this was made into a matte and composited over Mark Lenard's tear, producing a highlighted lighting effect which heightened the emotional impact of this crucial scene.

One of the third season's outstanding episodes, "Tin Man," involved a full Betazoid telepath and his relationship with the sentient spacecraft of the title; "Tin Man" itself was another superb model crafted by Greg Jein, Incorporated. Also on hand as the end of the third season approached was a new Enterprise model. This was the work of Greg Jein, constructed for Dan Curry and Robert Legato, the show's special effects wizards. Lighting for the new model was the work of Robert Legato's assistant, Gary Hutzel.

After supplanting Industrial Light and Magic early in the course of THE NEXT GENERATION's first season, Curry and Legato developed new and more flexible ways to present the Enterprise using digital visual compositing rather than optical film effects. Their approach makes it possible to add a theoretically limitless number of elements to a shot without any loss of image clarity. As the series proceeded, they built a library of shots which could easily be altered and reused without any risk of redundancy; this rather impressive library now contain hundreds of shots.

As for the new model, it was easier to use than the original six-footer, which was, however, the only model with hull separation capacity. The six-footer was also a very complex piece of lighting wiring; the new model simplified things considerably with a flexible neon system. (The windows and interior lights are actually visual effects composited on later in the shooting process.) The four-foot Enterprise also differed from the older models in that Greg Jein gave it a surface that was not smooth, but rather layered (think of a topographical map). This detail made the lighting on this model a good deal more interesting.

The third season finale, "The Best of Both Worlds, Part One," was the most expensive show of that season and easily the one with the most effects shots.

FOURTH SEASON

With the beginning of the fourth season, a whiz-bang sequel to the third season cliffhanger was certainly in order. The conclusion to "The Best of Both Worlds" called for something that hadn't been done since "Encounter At Farpoint." A saucer separation had not been utilized as a plot device since the pilot. The six foot model of the Enterprise was the only one built to have saucer separation capabilities. It was brought out of storage for Robert Legato's team to shoot in "The Best Of Both Worlds" and the cumbersomeness of it made for a difficult time. It just reinforced all of their feelings about why a smaller model worked better for their specific needs.

"The Best Of Both Worlds" featured a higher than normal amount of complicated optical effects. In the scene where three Martian probes attack the Borg ship, that shot involved several elements—the starfield, the three probes blowing up, the planet Mars and the Borg ship flying towards the camera and then away. Ten seconds of screen time for something that complex can take four to five days to shoot.

The fourth season of STAR TREK: THE NEXT GENERATION marked yet another move closer to the future for the effects on the series. The focus of THE NEXT GENERATION's post-production effort at the start of this season shifted to the new Digital Center in Edit Bay B at The Post Group's facilities. This move freed the show from the long-standing necessity of working with analog, one-inch tape. Now, THE NEXT GENERATION could go completely digital. Some of the equipment involved in the show is so advanced that it doesn't even have any directions from the factory.

The Post Group is in fact among the first people to actually employ this equipment. Among the many state-of-the-art devices in the world, there are only three Abekas A84s in existence— and The Post Group owns two of them. They also have a wealth of other digital compositing, computer imaging and recording devices, not to mention the vast array of hardware and software required to integrate all of this equipment. This includes the Quantel Mirage, a very useful tool that is employed frequently to create planets for the show. The Mirage has the ability to wrap flat images onto a sphere or other shape.

A DOWNWARD TURN

The generally high quality of the fourth season took a painful plunge downwards with "Night Terrors." Deanna Troi has allegedly terrifying but really lame-looking flying dreams. Michael Piller, somewhat apologetically, is on record as claiming that the show was weak because everyone was still getting their 'space legs' after taking time off for the Christmas season. Jonathan Frakes, not one to mince words, described Deanna's flying scenes as "shitty," and the episode itself as boring. Resident NEXT GENERATION special effects chief, Rob Legato, was a bit embarrassed by the effects involved but pointed out that flying never looks right. One can only hope that Marina Sirtis will never again be obliged to hang from wires as she did here.

"Identity Crisis," in which an alien virus transforms Geordi LaForge and another crew member into invisible alien beings, was highlighted by ultraviolet effects which were created by a company called Wildfire. Wildfire was also responsible for ultraviolet effects in BILL AND TED'S BOGUS JOURNEY, STAR TREK VI: THE UNDISCOVERED COUNTRY, and ALIEN 3.

Sometimes, special effects—in-camera effects, in this instance—are used to conceal something real rather than to create something unreal. "The Host" was filmed while Gates McFadden was pregnant. This obliged first-time NEXT GENERATION director Marvin V. Rush, to avoid showing her stomach by strategic camera placement or, as Jonathan Frakes succinctly put it, by filming her "from her boobs up." In one shot, McFadden is sitting on a piece of furniture; she begins to stand up, and Michael Dorn says something, prompting Patrick Stewart to move by her; the camera follows Stewart's turn as McFadden rises and leaves the shot. Thus, Rush showed her standing but managed to conceal her pregnancy by strategic placing of Stewart combined with camera movement designed to distract viewers from the fact that Stewart was being used as a decoy!

"Redemption" marked STAR TREK: THE NEXT GENERATION's liberation from stock movie footage of Klingon vessels, as a new top-of-the-line Klingon cruiser was unveiled in the fourth season's cliffhanger finale. By the end of the fourth season, effects supervisor Robert Legato had also directed two episodes: "Menage a Troi," and "The Nth Degree," which featured the return of Dwight Schultz as Ensign Reginald Barclay.

FIFTH SEASON

The fifth season of STAR TREK: THE NEXT GENERATION opened up with the concluding second half of "Redemption," which wrapped up things on the Klingon home world. The Great Hall of Klingon no longer existed as a full set. Only half of it survived from the Great Hall's first appearance in the "Sins of the Father," the third season episode which kicked off the classic Worf's Dishonor series. This was not an insurmountable problem. After half the shots for the Great Hall sequences were filmed, the set was completely redressed, and all the reverse angle shots were filmed against the same set doing double duty.

The episode "Disaster," featured Picard trapped the turbolift with a group of children. When they escape up the turbolift shaft, there is a shot in which Captain Picard looks down to see one of the children. Since the turbolift shaft does not exist as a full set but only as an eight-inch-diameter miniature, Dan Curry had to composite all these elements in the proper perspective. This was a tricky proposition further complicated by the fact that boy was wearing a blue costume, which made it necessary to shoot part of this sequence as a *green*-screen effect rather than the more common blue-screen.

"Disaster" also marked the on-screen debut of a new, more cramped Jeffries Tube set. A collapsible set, the Jeffries Tube is easily stored and just as easily hauled out for use. The Jeffries Tube, named after Matt Jeffries (the original production designer on the sixties STAR TREK) is an access tube through which people can climb to gain access to the inner workings of the Enterprise. Its most visible use in the fifth season was in "Disaster" and in "The Game."

Another fifth season episode, "Silicon Avatar" saw the return of the Crystalline Entity, with spanking new visual effects from Rob Legato's crack team. The Entity was far more convincing this time around than it was in the first season's "Datalore." This episode's external sequences representing a planet where a colony is to be established were shot at the Disney Ranch.

"Violations" was an intriguing episode to which director Robert Wiemer brought some unusual touches. Although the identity of the villain was pretty obvious, "Violations" was perhaps most interesting in that it offered some tantalizing glimpses into the personal past lives of some of the Enterprise crew. With Rick Berman's sanction, Robert Wiemer went well outside the show's usual visual format to create images of a romantic interlude between Deanna Troi and Riker, and of a young Beverly Crusher being taken to view her husband's body by a young (with hair) Jean-Luc Picard. Both sequences have a disjointed, disturbing quality which presages the intrusion of the psychic invader into these dream-like passages.

WORKING SMART

Eschewing the use of a total post-production, special-effects approach to these scenes, Wiemer attempted to do most of the work up front, as he shot the scenes. Most impressive was the Crusher/Picard sequence, which used wide-angle lenses and unusual camera movements to create a disjointed and apprehensive atmosphere. Movements in close-up might seem particularly odd because Wiemer actually had the two actors sit on a dolly; rather than walking, they were actually moved along by the dolly and filmed them from the chest up, creating a disturbing sense of "wrong" body movement reminiscent of some of the techniques used by Jean Cocteau in the underworld sequences of his classic black-and-white film ORPHEUS.

Some technical shots are more than ordinarily demanding. In the fifth season episode "A Matter Of Time," the special effects team was called upon to show the Enterprise cleansing a planet's atmosphere of smoke and ash particles. This required shooting liquid nitrogen and dry ice in a tank with hot water in order to get the equivalent of cloud movements which could then be manipulated in the context of the Enterprise. The flat atmosphere footage thus created was placed on digital videotape and transferred around the spherical shape of the planet in question at the Digital Magic facility.

Dan Curry was in charge of this effort, which also required three expensive matte paintings of wintery background scenery. Unfortunately, this episode's budget only allowed for *two* such matte paintings, which were created by Matt Stromberg and Sid Dutton at Illusion Arts. The third, therefore, was whipped up by Dan Curry, using still photographs of glaciers, altered with the DFX, in essence a computerized paint box, and this served quite admirably.

For "The First Duty," in which Wesley Crusher faces some serious trouble, the show went back to the Sepulveda Basin, which had served as the planet Edo in the first season clunker "Justice," in order to create a setting for Starfleet Academy. Production designer Richard James provided the mattes which altered the existing buildings and placed the Golden Gate Bridge in the background. One week after principle photography was completed, the entire area was flooded.

While the fifth season saw an upswing in location shooting, the infamous Planet Hell set of Paramount's Stage Sixteen did not go neglected. The exciting opening sequence of "Power Play," set on a storm-ravaged planet, involved a great deal of windblown sand, which also required constant makeup retouches for Marina Sirtis and the other actors involved, as the sand effectively pitted their makeup in no time at all.

WINDING UP THE SEASON

"Power Play" (to some a reworking of a TREK classic episode) gave Data, Troi and O'Brien a chance to be possessed by alien entities, and thereby gave them a shot at essaying radically different characters. (*This* evil Data, of course, had to be played differently than Lore.) For the scenes in which the sparkling lights representing the alien life forces entered or exited their hosts, Dan Curry avoided animation or motion control and instead worked up a video version of Noh puppeteering: dressed in black from head to toe, except for a green fluorescent mitten, with which he did the alien movements by hand, and then composited the imagery into the live action footage. "Power Play" was one of the most expensive episodes of the fifth season, which came as quite an embarrassment to its director, David Livingston who, as THE NEXT GENERATION's line producer, is usually in charge of keeping directors on schedule—and within the constraints of the show's budget.

"The Perfect Mate," in which Ferengi greed threatens an arranged political marriage and inadvertently provides an unwilling Picard with another strong romantic interest, called for the interstellar mail-order bride to be transported in a stasis cocoon, which Dan Curry created by dragging a silver blanket behind a rippled piece of shower glass, and then wrapping the effect (colored yellow) around a basic egg shape using the System-G.

For the revelation of the cocoon's contents, the actress involved lay on apple boxes in the shuttle bay set (the boxes were electronically removed later) and the cocoon was superimposed over her in post-production. Computer animation wipes "undid" the substance of the cocoon, revealing first the inner shell, which was "wrapped" around the form of the actress, again using the System-G. The motion here was actually created by simply spraying a piece of glass with a common garden hose, shooting this with an eight-millimeter video system and, as usual, "wrapping" the effect with the System-G.

Although the fifth season of THE NEXT GENERATION was easily the most erratic season of all, often plunging close to first-season lack of quality, it also produced some superb episodes, one of which, "The Inner Light," was directed by special effects producer Peter Lauritson. This episode also came in seven minutes over standard length, so Lauritson also gained some crucial editing experience on the episode, in which Picard relives an alien's entire life. With Lauritson and Robert Legato having directed episodes, it should come as no surprise that Dan Curry, too, is eyeballing the possibility of expanding his NEXT GENERATION activities to a stint behind the camera.

The final episode of the fifth season, "Time's Arrow," was, in what now seems an established tradition, a cliffhanger. At first it looked like it was going to turn into the long dreaded "Data's Brain" of THE NEXT GENERATION, but it proved to be something far better. The scenes set in Nineteenth-Century San Francisco were actually shot in downtown Los Angeles and at a mansion in Pasadena.

After five years on the air, more than five hundred special visual effects have been created for THE NEXT GENERATION, which allows the reusing of some shots and even compositing shots together. For instance, a scene of the Enterprise can be combined with a previously recorded image of a Romulan ship to create a completely new shot of the two ships in the same frame. The sixth season of STAR TREK: THE NEXT GENERATION, already underway, promises yet another year of new effects to add to that bag of tricks. Not content to sit on their laurels, all involved in this show's special effects— Peter Lauritson, Robert Legato, Dan Curry, Ron Moore and all the others— promise to continue to bring their bast to their task of bringing the Twenty-fourth Century of STAR TREK: THE NEXT GENERATION to vivid life in our own time, the Twentieth Century.

Glossary of Terms

Occasionally you may come across a technical term with which you are unfamiliar. While these terms are generally defined within the context in which they're presented, once in awhile they aren't, or else they were defined in an earlier chapter you perhaps skipped over. The following should encompass any such unusual terms you encounter in this book.

ANIMATION STAND

Originally developed for photographing animated cartoons, it has been adapted for other motion picture animation applications. It consists of an animation camera capable of photographing film one frame at a time. There is also an easel or stand which holds the artwork or item being shot so that it is held rigidly in place. The camera can be moved in relation to the art and the artwork can also be moved in relation to the camera.

BLUE-SCREEN

Blue screen photography involves filming foreground elements (actors or model work) in front a screen which is illuminated a very intense blue in color. The color negatives obtained from this can be used to create mattes. The mattes will be composited with background plates shot separately.

COMPOSITE

This involves combining two or more images shot separately so that two or more separate pieces of film are combined to create a combined image. Thus all of the elements combined form a single image, such as a spaceship in front of a planet.

COMPUTER GRAPHICS

Images generated entirely on a computer using complicated paint programs. The representation of the Genesis Effect viewed early in THE WRATH OF KHAN is a one-hundred percent computer generated image. Such an image can be combined with live action, as in STAR TREK VI when the globules of blood are shown drifting in the weightlessness of the Klingon ship during the assassination sequence.

DYKSTRAFLEX

This is a motion-control camera system developed by John Dykstra for Industrial Light & Magic during the production of STAR WARS. John Dykstra supervised the design and construction of a special camera which allowed the camera to move on seven different axis of movement and tied it to a computer so that the camera could duplicate complex movements over and over again electronically. The camera is now often just referred to as the "Flex."

EFFECTS ANIMATION

This is used to add such elements as rain, lightning etc. to a scene which is either previously photographed live action or a miniature.

FORCED PERSPECTIVE

This can be done either with miniatures or with backdrop paintings on a sound stage. In a miniature, the background will be made on a much smaller scale from the portion immediately in front of it. In the two-dimensional medium of film, the background when photographed appears to be much further away from the camera than it really is.

HANGING MINIATURE

This is when a miniature is suspended between the camera lens and a full size set so that the miniature and the full size set combine on film to create a single image. When done correctly, the foreground hanging miniature appears on film to be part of the full size set and doesn't appear to be a miniature at all.

IN-THE-CAMERA EFFECTS

Done to save complicated post-production special effects, a single strip of film is masked off and then exposed more than once. This is sometimes done to film an actor playing a dual role so that he can appear to be talking to his double in the same scene on the same set.

MATTE

This is a mask which blocks off a portion of a photographic image in the shape of that mask. It is used in such things as adding special effects to the view screen on the Enterprise bridge or in the old TV series it was part of the Transporter effect used to added the sparkle.

MATTE PAINTING

Artwork sometimes (but not always) painted on glass. It is designed to be shot and added to a live action plate to enlarge on a previously photographed scene, such as the Tram Station at the beginning of STAR TREK—THE MOTION PICTURE. A small portion of the station was live action filmed on a sound stage. The rest was a painting filmed separately and combined with the live action footage to create a single image. Such paintings are rendered so realistically that they are not always recognizable as paintings.

MECHANICAL EFFECTS

` This means the same thing as practical effects or physical effects. These are live action effects staged on a set or location and filmed in a live action setting. They can be mechanical devices or else simple explosions.

MINIATURE

A model built to represent something larger, such as a city, or something imaginary, like a space craft. They tend to be a fraction of the size of the object they represent, but can be up to several feet long in some cases.

MORPHING

A type of computer graphics in which an image, such as a person, can be scanned into a computer for the purpose of combining that person's filmed image with other filmed images and blending them seamlessly. Used in STAR TREK VI: THE UNDISCOVERED

COUNTRY when Iman turned into Kirk.

MOTION CONTROL

Describes a camera system which is generally linked to a computer. This camera system allows the camera's movements to be recorded by the computer so that the camera can duplicate those movements exactly, and if necessary, over and over again.

MULTIPLANE CAMERA

This involves using an animation stand so that it can shoot more than one plane of artwork simultaneously. It creates as illusion of depth so that even in the two-dimensional medium of film, the image has a foreground, middleground and background and may appear to have been photographed from life.

OPTICAL EFFECTS

Also known as visual effects or even photographic effects. This refers to the wide array of image manipulations and techniques available through the aid of various optical systems and special effects cameras.

OPTICAL PRINTER

This device consists of a projector and a camera positioned so that their lenses face each other. This projector can project its image into the optical system of the camera. The optical printer allows for the combination of mattes (called composites) as well as such film techniques as fades and wipes.

PLATE

This is a piece of film which contains the filmed background element which when combined with another piece of film forms a composite.

PYROTECHNICS

The type of physical effects which involve fires and explosions. It has been expanded to include special visual effects involving explosions achieved through complicated means.

ROTOSCOPING

This involves projecting a filmed image one frame at a time onto a surface so that the image can be traced and outlined. The traced images can be turned into mattes for achieving complicated effects, usually involved with combining special effects with live action.

TRAVELING MATTES

These are mattes, or masks, which change from frame to frame and are very complicated and time consuming to accomplish.

TREK: THE UNAUTHORIZED BEHIND-THE-SCENES STORY OF THE NEXT GENERATION

James VanHise

This book chronicles the Trek mythos as it continues on T.V. in "Star Trek: The Next Generation," telling the often fascinating conflict filled story of the behind-the-scenes struggles between Roddenberry and the creative staff. It includes a special section on "Star Trek: Deep Space Nine," a spin-off of "The Next Generation," which will begin syndication in early 1993.

$14.95.....160 Pages
ISBN 1-55698-321-2

THE NEW TREK ENCYCLOPEDIA

John Peel with Scott Nance

Everything anyone might want to know about the Star Trek series of television shows and movies is conveniently compiled into one volume in *The New Trek Encyclopedia.*

This detailed volume covers the original T.V. series, all six feature films, "Star Trek: The Next Generation," and the animated show. It provides descriptions, explanations, and important details of every alien race, monster, planet, spaceship, weapon, and technical device to appear in all the shows— all listed in alphabetical order for easy reference. It also includes every person who worked on the shows or movies!

$19.95.....300 Pages
ISBN 1-55698-350-6

COUCH POTATO INC.   5715 N. Balsam Rd   Las Vegas, NV 89130   (702)658-2090

Use Your Credit Card 24 HRS — Order toll Free From: **(800)444-2524** Ext 67

BORING, BUT NECESSARY ORDERING INFORMATION

Payment:

Use our new 800 # and pay with your credit card or send check or money order directly to our address. All payments must be made in U.S. funds and please do not send cash.

Shipping:

We offer several methods of shipment. Sometimes a book can be delayed if we are temporarily out of stock. You should note whether you prefer us to ship the book as soon as available, send you a merchandise credit good for other goodies, or send your money back immediately.

Normal Post Office: $3.75 for the first book and $1.50 for each additional book. These orders are filled as quickly as possible. Shipments normally take 5 to 10 days, but allow up to 12 weeks for delivery.

Special UPS 2 Day Blue Label Service or Priority Mail: Special service is available for desperate Couch Potatoes. These books are shipped within 24 hours of when we receive the order and normally take 2 to 3 three days to get to you. The cost is $10.00 for the first book and $4.00 each additional book .

Overnight Rush Service: $20.00 for the first book and $10.00 each additional book.

U.s. Priority Mail: $6.00 for the first book and $3.00.each additional book.

Canada And Mexico: $5.00 for the first book and $3.00 each additional book.

Foreign: $6.00 for the first book and $3.00 each additional book.

Please list alternatives when available and please state if you would like a refund or for us to backorder an item if it is not in stock.

COUCH POTATO INC.   5715 N. Balsam Rd   Las Vegas, NV 89130   (702)658-2090

Use Your Credit Card 24 HRS — Order toll Free From: **(800)444-2524** Ext 67

ORDER FORM

_____ Trek Crew Book $9.95
_____ Best Of Enterprise Incidents $9.95
_____ Trek Fans Handbook $9.95
_____ Trek: The Next Generation $14.95
_____ The Man Who Created Star Trek: $12.95
_____ 25th Anniversary Trek Tribute $14.95
_____ History Of Trek $14.95
_____ The Man Between The Ears $14.95
_____ Trek: The Making Of The Movies $14.95
_____ Trek: The Lost Years $12.95
_____ Trek: The Unauthorized Next Generation $14.95
_____ New Trek Encyclopedia $19.95
_____ Making A Quantum Leap $14.95
_____ The Unofficial Tale Of Beauty And The Beast $14.95
_____ Complete Lost In Space $19.95
_____ ..doctor Who Encyclopedia: Baker $19.95
_____ Lost In Space Tribute Book $14.95
_____ Lost In Space With Irwin Allen $14.95
_____ Doctor Who: Baker Years $19.95
_____ Doctor Who: Pertwee Years $19.95
_____ Batmania Ii $14.95
_____ The Green Hornet $14.95 _____ Special Edition $16.95

_____ Number Six: The Prisoner Book $14.95
_____ Gerry Anderson: Supermarionation $17.95
_____ Addams Family Revealed $14.95
_____ Bloodsucker: Vampires At The Movies $14.95
_____ Dark Shadows Tribute $14.95
_____ Monsterland Fear Book $14.95
_____ The Films Of Elvis $14.95
_____ The Woody Allen Encyclopedia $14.95
_____ Paul Mccartney: 20 Years On His Own $9.95
_____ Yesterday: My Life With The Beatles $14.95
_____ Fab Films Of The Beatles $14.95
_____ 40 Years At Night: The Tonight Show $14.95
_____ Exposing Northern Exposure $14.95
_____ The La Lawbook $14.95
_____ Cheers: Where Everybody Knows Your Name $14.95
_____ SNL! The World Of Saturday Night Live $14.95
_____ The Rockford Phile $14.95
_____ Encyclopedia Of Cartoon Superstars $14.95
_____ How To Create Animation $14.95
_____ How To Draw Art For Comic Books $14.95
_____ King And Barker:an Illustrated Guide $14.95
_____ King And Barker: An Illustrated Guide II $14.95

100% Satisfaction Guaranteed.

We value your support. You will receive a full refund as long as the copy of the book you are not happy with is received back by us in reasonable condition. No questions asked, except we would like to know how we failed you. Refunds and credits are given as soon as we receive back the item you do not want.

NAME:_____

STREET:_____

CITY:_____

STATE:_____

ZIP:_____

TOTAL:_____ SHIPPING_____

SPFX

SEND TO: Pioneer Books, Inc. 5715 N. Balsam Rd., Las Vegas, NV 89130

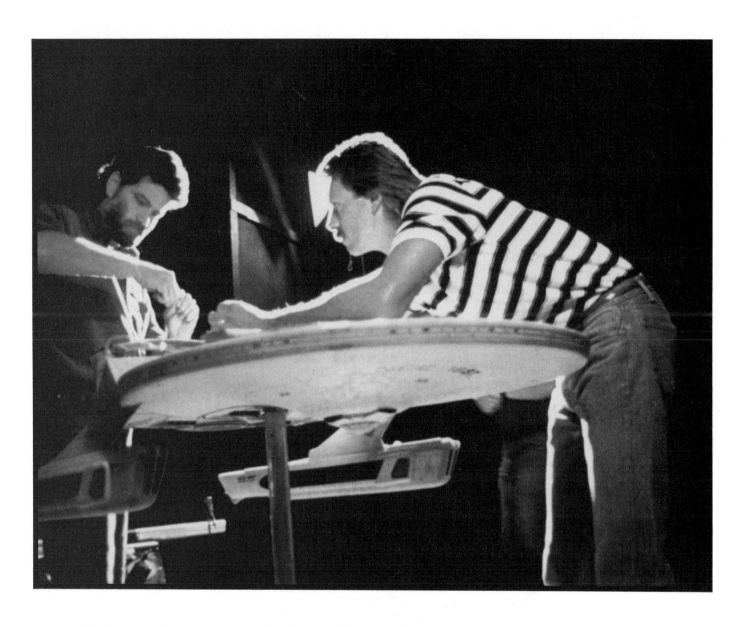

The Reliant under construction for STAR TREK II: THE WRATH OF KHAN.

THE SPECIAL EFFECTS OF TREK

By way of an introduction . . .
THE AGE OF SPECIAL EFFECTS

A special effect is any technique that creates an illusion of reality. Since no one can go into outer space to film the adventures of twenty-third century heroes, they have to fake it. The methods for achieving this have become both a science and an art.

Nearly thirty years of special effects history is what you have when you examine STAR TREK. From Matt Jeffries, Mike Minor, Wah Chang and Linwood Dunn who worked on the original television version of STAR TREK, up through Douglas Trumbull, John Dykstra, Syd Mead, Greg Jein, Brick Price, Andrew Probert and the other three hundred technicians who worked long house to make STAR TREK—THE MOTION PICTURE everything that it could technically be when it hit theater screens in 1979. Through all of them we can see not only how the importance of special effects to STAR TREK grew between the end of the series in 1969 and the release of STAR TREK—THE MOTION PICTURE in 1979, but also the strides made in the field itself. What was actually technologically possible changed in that one decade, and motion pictures changed dramatically along with it.

Coming in the wake of STAR WARS meant that STAR TREK itself would have to change to meet the perceived demands of the movie-going audience. In 1977 special effects rose from being something of obscure interest to a few enthusiasts to an industry of mammoth proportions. Budgets swelled along with the perceptions of what a film had to deliver, and riding the crest of this, then and now, has been Industrial Light & Magic. Founded by George Lucas when he made STAR WARS, ILM's name has been on some of the most technologically impressive motion pictures of the eighties and nineties. Their work has graced four of the six STAR TREK motion pictures, and their innovations continue to impress theater-going audiences.

In STAR TREK II: THE WRATH OF KHAN we saw a state-of-the-art space battle and the creation of a planet.

In STAR TREK III: THE SEARCH FOR SPOCK we saw technology pushed further to show the destruction of a series icon along with the end of the planet those special effects had given birth to. What special effects can create, so can they destroy.

STAR TREK IV: THE VOYAGE HOME presented a future which wasn't as perfect as we'd been led to believe, as it lacked a living creature which only the twentieth century (and more special effects) could provide.

STAR TREK V: THE FINAL FRONTIER has a really terrific looking Klingon Bird of Prey, and special effects showed that even God isn't what he used to be.

STAR TREK VI: THE UNDISCOVERED COUNTRY presented special effects elements which showed how the industry continues to evolve. Not only did it use morphing, presenting images considered impossible to convincingly achieve just a decade before, but also employed computer imaging in strange new ways which were a wonder to behold.

And over the last five years, STAR TREK: THE NEXT GENERATION has once again presented a steady diet of special effects delivered on a weekly basis, demonstrating the possibilities available with the burgeoning field of video technology.

The work of many technicians is explored in this book, and through their experiences we learn about the nature of special effects, how they are first visualized and the stages they go through before they are even put on film. It is a world of technological wonders which in thirty years has advanced to the point where virtually anything which can be imagined can be filmed—if you have the time and the money to realize that goal.

Each chapter presents a detailed behind-the-scenes account of what went into the demanding and inventive processes involved in rendering the imaginative into a believable form. From the earliest forms of the Enterprise to the latest presentation of that venerable spacecraft as it enters warp drive in a manner which would have been impossible to film in 1966. All levels of special effects are examined, from preparation to conclusion, and they're presented in a manner which the reader can not only understand and appreciate, but perhaps in so doing capture some of the sense of wonder that those effects generate when we see them on the screen.

—JAMES VAN HISE